D1118060

BERNARD OF CLAIRVAUX

THE CROSSROAD SPIRITUAL LEGACY SERIES
Edited by John Farina

The Rule of Benedict: Insights for the Ages
    by Joan Chittister, O.S.B.

Ignatius Loyola: Spiritual Exercises
    by Joseph A. Tetlow, S.J.

Francis de Sales: Introduction to the Devout Life
and Treatise on the Love of God
    by Wendy M. Wright

Teresa of Avila: Mystical Writings
    by Tessa Bielecki

St. Francis of Assisi: Writings for a Gospel Life
    by Regis J. Armstrong, O.F.M. Cap.

Augustine: Major Writings
    by Benedict J. Groeschel, C.S.R.

Hildegard: Prophet of the Cosmic Christ
    by Renate Craine

Karl Rahner: Mystic of Everyday Life
    by Harvey D. Egan

Thomas Aquinas: Spiritual Master
    by Robert Barron

C.S. Lewis: Spirituality for Mere Christians
    by William Griffin

Anselm: The Joy of Faith
    by William H. Shannon

Dante Alighieri: Divine Comedy, *Divine Spirituality*
    by Robert Royal

John of the Cross: Doctor of Light and Love
    by Kieran Kavanaugh, O.C.D.

Bonaventure: Mystical Writings
    by Zachary Hayes, O.F.M.

BERNARD OF CLAIRVAUX

ESSENTIAL WRITINGS

Dennis E. Tamburello, O.F.M.

A Crossroad Book
The Crossroad Publishing Company
New York

The Crossroad Publishing Company
481 Eighth Avenue, New York, NY 10001

Printed in the United States of America

Library of Congress Cataloging-in-Publication Data

Tamburello, Dennis E., 1953-
    Bernard of Clairvaux / Dennis E. Tamburello.
       p.   cm.
    Includes bibliographical references.
    ISBN 0-8245-2516-7 (alk. paper)
    1. Bernard, of Clairvaux, Saint, 1090 or 91-1153. I. Title.
  BX4700.B5 T35 2000
  271'.1202—dc21

                                        00-009491

1 2 3 4 5 6 7 8 9 10   04 03 02 01 00

I dedicate this book with love to my mother,

Doris C. Tamburello,

*whose devotion to Christ and to Mary
would make Bernard proud.*

Contents

Foreword

Bernard of Clairvaux in one of his most famous writings described the union between God and humanity as a kiss. He wrote of love in the twelfth century when many like the Jews in the Kabbalah movement, the Sufi mystics like Ibn 'Arabi, and the humanist poets of Europe were suffused with love. For Bernard, love was not the scholastic virtue of charity but a passion, a burning desire, an unmatched sweetness, a taste, a touch, a kiss.

Such was the instinct of this man, known to the church as the *doctor mellifluus*, that his most famous work was a commentary on the great love poem of the Bible, the Song of Songs. But unlike earlier commentaries on the Song, such as Origen's or Gregory of Nyssa's, Bernard stressed that carnal love cannot be denied but must be redirected to the sensible or carnal love of Christ's humanity. Only by loving Christ's humanity could we begin to love his divinity. Loving Christ in his humanity could be so vivid that it could drive out the taste for illicit loves that kept us trapped in our deformity.

It is not for nothing that the great Florentine bard of love, Dante, gave Bernard a preeminent place in the pilgrim's ascent to Paradise. After Virgil and Beatrice could lead him no further, it was Bernard who brought him to the ultimate vision of the Trinity.

Bernard was not only a writer on the spiritual life, he was also the foremost spokesman for the revival of monastic life known as Cistercianism. He entered the monastery of Cîteaux in 1113 at the age of twenty-three. The Cistercians were a reform movement within the Benedictines that stressed a return to a more rigorous observance of the Rule of Benedict. They insisted on supporting themselves through manual labor and went about founding new monasteries with a missionary fervor. One of those new foundations was in the valley of Clairvaux, near Aube, France. Only two years after entering the new community, Bernard was named abbot of Clairvaux.

The goal of the new movement was to create a setting in which persons redeemed by Christ could live out the full expression of their humanity. They would be motivated to ignore the temptations of the flesh, to eschew worldly power, and to walk in simple humility not by a strict rule and stern taskmasters but by love. Bernard became the great intellectual and spiritual leader of the movement.

But how can we appropriate Bernard's vision for today? Certainly on its face its form seems remote and uninviting. Who would readily exchange the comforts of the modern city for the austerity of rural living in which one was forced to scratch out a living from the ground, owning nothing for oneself?

The key to learning from Bernard today is understanding his connection to the world, not his renunciation of it. He speaks of an optimistic view of human nature—optimistic because it has been redeemed by union with God's nature in the Incarnation. That sanguine view means that one can love the creation as a work of God and work for the reformation of the world. We are invited to a cooperation with God in the ongoing work of making the world.

This, I would suggest, is a vision of humanity much like

that defined in *Gaudium et Spes.* It is what is behind Pope Paul VI's civilization of love, and so much of John Paul II's vision of evangelizing culture. Yet that vision of humanity has done little to give birth to a vital lay spirituality within the Catholic Church. Too often lay Catholics are beset by ultramontanist fantasies of an infallible church, led by perfect priests whose characters have been transformed by reason of holy orders and now partake in a quality of holiness that those sullied by their worldly contacts can never experience. Thus discharged from the call to radical conversion, many are content to let the clergy live out the gospel while they passively partake of just enough religion to ease the conscience. In Bernard, however, there is a start that could foster a fresh rethinking of the relationship between body and soul, sensuality and charity, and church and world. That task would not be easy, for Bernard cannot simply be transplanted into our age whole. But there is here a beginning that in its style and substance is more compelling than the current versions of neo-Thomism being offered.

In this Spiritual Legacy volume, Dennis Tamburello offers us a skillful guide to beginning a dialog with Bernard. He presents the necessary background to understand medieval monasticism, Bernard's thought, and the role of the church in society. He also invites us to study the scripture with Bernard, to pray with him, and to long with him for the kiss of God. May we, in yearning for that kiss, find in our day a path to the reform of society that the monks of Cîteaux worked so tirelessly for in their own time.

John Farina

Introduction

It may seem strange that a Franciscan, and not a Cistercian, is writing this introduction to the writings of Bernard of Clairvaux. I am well aware of the privilege that this is, and I am grateful to the Crossroad Publishing Company, especially the editors of the Spiritual Legacy series, for entrusting the task to me. I consider myself to be not so much an expert on Bernard as an ongoing student of his. After many years of studying various aspects of his life and work, I find that the well of his wisdom runs very deep indeed, and I wonder if I will ever learn enough about him. I hope to share some of the excitement of Bernard studies with the readers of this volume.

Historically, to be sure, there is some justification for a Franciscan to be writing about Bernard. The Cistercian order pioneered many of the aspects of religious life that would later also become trademarks of Franciscanism: poverty and simplicity of life, a rejection of worldly economic standards, a passionate devotion to Christ, and an organization that balances centralized authority with local autonomy. Whether the orders have adequately sustained all of these features over the long haul is another question, one that I would hesitate to answer for the Franciscans, let alone the Cistercians. In any event, so much of Bernard's spirituality has resonated with my own life as a friar that I have tended to see Bernard as a kind of "honorary uncle" to Franciscans.

Much of the manuscript of this book was written during a sabbatical semester that I spent at the Franciscan friary in Freiburg, Germany. I am grateful to the friars of the Fulda Province for their continued hospitality and fraternal support. Both of my other books were also in large part completed here.

At Crossroad Publishing, I am grateful to Bob Heller, who first suggested I write for the series and was immensely helpful in working out the details of the contract, and to John Farina, Paul McMahon, and Gwendolyn Herder, who helped me to see the manuscript through to completion. I am most thankful for their patience with me, as the distractions of my other commitments resulted in the deadline being pushed back several times.

I also wish to thank my colleagues, students, and the friars at Siena College, where I am happy to live and work. I tip my hat especially to the library staff, who always have been so helpful when I have needed to locate hard-to-find materials.

Finally, I thank once again my family for their unflagging support of my academic endeavors even when they have not been able to relate easily to the topics on which I write.

Abbreviations

Full publication information is given in the selected bibliography on page 158. Texts of Bernard and the Rule of St. Benedict are cited by chapter/section or letter/section numbers.

CO   *On Conversion (De conversione)*

DC   *Five Books on Consideration (De consideratione)*

DD   *On Loving God (De diligendo Deo)*

DG   *On Grace and Free Choice (De gratia et libero arbitrio)*

GH   *The Steps of Humility and Pride (De gradibus humilitatis et superbiae)*

HL   *Homilies in Praise of the Blessed Virgin Mary (Homilia in laudibus virginis matris)*

LB   *The Letters of St. Bernard of Clairvaux*

RB   *The Rule of St. Benedict*

SC   *Sermons on the Song of Songs (Sermones super Cantica)*

Other texts are cited by page numbers.

VP   *First Life of St. Bernard (Vita prima Bernardi)*

CS   *Bernard of Clairvaux and the Cistercian Spirit*

HC   *The Story of Abelard's Adversities (Historia Calamitatum)*

IR   *The Cistercians: Ideals and Reality*

LL   *The Love of Learning and the Desire for God*

LW   *Bernhard von Clairvaux: Leben und Werk des berühmten Zisterziensers*

NCE   *New Catholic Encyclopedia*

RW   *Bernhard von Clairvaux: Rezeption und Wirkung im Mittelalter und in der Neuzeit*

Chapter 1

Bernard's World: The Historical Context

Bernard of Clairvaux (1090–1153) was a man of unique personality, living during a time of great transition in the history of the church. In order to understand him, we must know something about developments in the medieval church, especially after 1000 C.E. In this chapter, we will explore the historical context of Bernard's life.

The Church, the State, and Monasticism

Although Bernard is well known in the Christian world as a spiritual writer, he was also a prominent statesman for his day. In fact, he went so far as to take it upon himself to give advice to the pope! But, we might ask, why would a person living in a monastery want to get involved in the church's public affairs? Aren't monks supposed to stay in their monasteries and pray? And why would a pope need or want the advice of a monk like Bernard?

Simple answers cannot be given to these questions. Both the church in general, and monastic life in particular, developed in complex and sometimes unexpected ways over the centuries. In studying the history of Christianity, I have often found it helpful to think in terms of basic *tensions* that seem to be a constant challenge to the church. The history of the church can be seen as the story of how these tensions are lived out at different times and by different groups within the community of faith. Taking this approach to church history, one sees problems and crises in the church as the result of one or more imbalances that develop as it tries to walk the tightrope between extreme positions.

Perhaps most relevant to our study of Bernard is the tension that has always existed in the church between its relation to the world and its relation to God: more specifically, between its focus on worldly affairs and its focus on the affairs of heaven or the spiritual life. It was this very tension that gave rise to monasticism to begin with and that contributed both to its successes and failures. As we shall see, Bernard of Clairvaux exemplified the tension in striking ways.

During the first few centuries of Christianity's history, the church lived in almost constant fear of the Roman Empire. Christianity was a new religion, and as soon as it was recognized as such, that is, as soon as it clearly distinguished itself from the Judaism from which it arose, it was immediately declared illegal and an enemy of the empire. The intensity with which the Christians were persecuted varied from emperor to emperor. The persecution was fierce and virtually constant between 250 and 311 C.E.

During this period, Christians dealt with the God/world tension by seeing themselves as "in" the world but not "of" the world. They knew that as followers of Jesus they had to be engaged in the world but in a different way than their contemporaries. Jesus had commanded them to proclaim the reign of God, particularly by being women and men "for others," pouring out their lives in service as Jesus himself had done. Christians became involved in various kinds of what we would call "social service"—feeding the hungry, caring for the sick, and so on—in effect, filling an important gap in an empire that was not particularly known for being socially conscious.

However, it was extremely difficult to live such a life and not be noticed. Knowing that their very existence was deemed illegal by the empire, Christians in general kept a low profile, so as not to draw attention to themselves unnecessarily. Indeed, the community of believers was suspicious of those who seemed to be a bit too eager for martyrdom. Nevertheless, it was inevitable that many of them would be apprehended, tried, and executed. Because Christians refused to offer sacrifice to the Roman gods, the official protectors of the empire, they were regarded as enemies of the state.

Not surprisingly, persecution was at its peak when the empire was in crisis. Christians became a convenient scapegoat on whom to blame the empire's problems. Some Christians caved in under pressure and saved their lives by offering sacrifice to the Roman gods or by obtaining fraudulent certificates that "proved" that they had done so. Many others went to their deaths. During this period, to be a perfect Christian was to be a martyr.

All this was to change with the rise of the Emperor Constantine to power. In 313, he promulgated the famous Edict of Milan, which effectively recognized the Roman Empire's inability to wipe Christianity out, and declared that Christians—and indeed all other people in the empire—were free to worship as they chose. Constantine, however, went further than this. He arranged for the return of properties that had been taken from Christians and became the church's biggest benefactor, even donating money for a basilica in Rome. (This basilica no longer stands, but the basilica of St. Peter was erected on the same site.) Constantine declared himself to be a Christian and clearly favored the Christian religion, but he did not outlaw any other religion.

By the end of the fourth century, Emperor Theodosius had declared Christianity to be the official state religion, displacing the old Roman cult of the gods—the same gods whom Christians died refusing to worship just decades earlier. Before it was illegal to *be* a Christian; now it was illegal *not* to be one. Theoretically, Jews were exempt from this, although in practice they suffered much under the "Christian" empire.

The impact of these changes on the Christian community should not be underestimated. Before the fourth century C.E., conversion to Christianity was a dangerous decision that could lead to an early and grizzly death. Now it became a social convention: for the vast majority of people, to be a member of the empire was to be a Christian. Before, Christians saw themselves as "in" the world but not "of" the world. Now it appeared that they could have their cake and eat it too: they could follow Jesus publicly and still be full citizens of the Roman Empire.

To some people, this state of affairs spelled the end of the Christian ideal. Since it was now easy to be a Christian, they believed that the focus on God and the reign of God was sure to take a back seat to engagement in worldly affairs. It was largely this shift in the balance of the God/world tension that gave rise to the monastic impulse. Many who sought a more perfect way of following Jesus withdrew from the general society to live an intense life of prayer and devotion. The first people to do this were solitaries; soon thereafter, a communal form of life developed, which is what we usually describe as "monasticism." During the age of persecution, to be a perfect Christian was to be a martyr; over a period of time, monastic or "religious" life replaced martyrdom as the way of following Christ more perfectly.

Religious Life in the Middle Ages

Monastic life, then, began in part as a reaction against the kind of complacent, easy Christianity that became possible at the time of Constantine. To counteract the worldliness of this new, official state Christianity, hermits and monks focused their attention on the gospel and sought a life of total devotion to God.

Such is the essential characteristic of the monastic impulse: the desire for God, accompanied by detachment from the world and from sin. Monks and nuns desired to return to that more primitive form of Christian experience, when Christians were "in" the world only in the most marginal way and were definitely not "of" it. Indeed, withdrawal from the world was seen as a prerequisite for keeping one's attention totally focused on God. In practice, however, monasteries often came to reflect medieval society more than they stood apart from it.

Some of the earliest monks and solitaries are described in contemporary sources as people who were engaged in a dramatic struggle against evil and self-will. St. Athanasius's *Life of Antony* is a good illustration of this. Antony, who withdrew to the desert and not just to the outskirts of the city as other solitaries did, is said to have engaged in brutal combats with the devil, both psychological and physical. Other accounts tell us of monks who led lives of rigorous mortification to extinguish the passions of the flesh. Thus we hear of monks standing naked in pools of ice-cold water, and of solitaries like Simon the Stylite, who lived on top of a post.

Then St. Benedict came along, who founded the type of monasticism that Bernard would later embrace, though in a revised form. Benedict had a different idea. He wrote a Rule for his monks (a set of guidelines for their communal life) that was remarkably detailed and complete. Provisions were made for every conceivable aspect of daily life. One might expect that such a regulated life would be extremely demanding. Yet Benedict himself stated that he wanted to set down a rule that contained "nothing harsh, nothing burdensome" (RB, prologue). For all its exactitude, it was written with a tone of compassion and moderation.

For example, in chapter 29 of the Rule, where Benedict speaks of brothers being dismissed from the monastery, he allows for a repentant brother to be readmitted to the community as many as three times. In chapter 39, he discusses the preparation of food and states that at least two kinds of cooked food should be available at meals, so that brothers who cannot eat certain foods will have a choice. In chapter 43, Benedict prescribes a penance for those who come late for Vigils; he defines "late" as arriving after the "Glory Be to the Father" at the end of Psalm 94. But he begins by exhorting the brothers to pray that prayer "quite deliberately and slowly," to give latecomers a chance to avoid the penalty.

Everything in Benedict's rule ultimately served one goal: the search for God. Most people, if they know nothing else about medieval monasticism, know that the monasteries were largely responsible for the transmission of ancient manuscripts down through the ages. Monks were the ones who copied the great texts of antiquity and preserved them for the future—in an age when there were no computers or printing presses. It is true that the monasteries were centers of learning. The monks studied diligently the scriptures, the writings of the early fathers of the church, and classical literature, in that order of importance (LL).

But these things were not studied purely for intellectual knowledge, as they could be, for example, in the medieval universities. All learning was at the service of love and devotion to God. Reading and studying were seen as nothing less than an act of prayer, as another means of fanning the flames of desire for God. As St. Gregory the Great, who began as a Benedictine monk and later became pope from 590–604, put it: love itself is knowledge. This equation of true knowledge with the love of God is a theme that is very strong in the writings of Bernard. It later becomes part of the legacy of the Protestant Reformation, which is especially interesting, given the clear aversion to monastic life that is expressed in the writings of major Reformers like Luther and Calvin.

Monasticism has often been accused of a certain elitism, of holding up an ideal for the Christian life that only some people, namely monks and nuns, can realize. I am not sure that monasticism can be entirely defended against this charge. Ideally, the single-minded devotion of the monks was supposed to be a witness to the world, a reminder of the priority that should be utmost in the lives of *all* Christians: the desire for God. However, one does detect a judgment in many classic monastic writings, including those of St. Bernard, that the monastery was really the best milieu for working out one's salvation, for it was believed that only there could one be free from the distractions of the world, which pulled people away from God. We will return to this issue in later chapters.

It was precisely the monasteries' role as witnesses to the

world that caused their separation from the world to be gradually diluted over time. The monks were well aware of the need to work for the salvation of all people, and the church at large was more than happy to tap the resources of the monasteries to promote the Christian life. Many monasteries also came to enjoy the patronage of lay rulers, and so developed not only into great centers of learning and devotion, but also often into centers of wealth and even opulence. Monasticism, which began as a kind of reform movement within the church, itself came to be in dire need of reform. The Cistercian movement arose out of the desire to return medieval monasticism to its roots, to go back to the pure living of the gospel.

Benedictines and Cistercians

By the time Bernard was born, a spirit of reform had already been burning in monasticism for about two centuries. Much of this reform ran parallel to the papal attempt, which reached its zenith in Pope Gregory VII (1073–1085), to restore the church's independence from medieval society. On the one hand, there was a great deal of secular influence in the church. During the feudal period, when the structures of church and society had become unstable, a situation developed whereby lay rulers were essentially appointing and installing ("investing") church officials. It must be admitted that this system gave the church some very good leaders and indeed may have saved the hierarchy from self-destruction at times, as various families feuded with each other for control. But it was clear that this practice of "lay investiture" was a threat to the church's autonomy; ironically, the practice produced church leaders who were strong and stable enough to challenge it. On the other hand, the church was also involving itself in the affairs of the world, as evidenced by the problem of simony, the buying and selling of leadership positions in the church.

Once again, the tension between being "in" the world and being "of" the world was manifesting itself. As the church worked to reassert its independence from the world, so too did monks begin to look at how worldly their lifestyles had become. They came to believe that the solution to this dilemma was a return to the apostolic life as it was lived in the primitive church, with an emphasis on poverty and eremitism, that is, living as hermits (IR, 5).

We have already noted that early monasticism (before St. Benedict) was characterized by many who lived as solitaries. Thus, monastic renewal in this period was motivated by developments that really *preceded* Benedict's Rule. As the great Cistercian scholar Louis Lekai puts it, "The common denominator of all eleventh-century reforming efforts was the desire to establish a life of heroic mortifications spent in retirement from all worldy entanglements" (IR, 10).

But many reform movements of this period did not have staying power. Unlike Benedict, whose Rule made concessions to human frailty, some of the new reformers had no tolerance for moderation. Lekai notes, "They refused to recognize the truth that institutions to endure must take into account the limitations of average men, not the ambitions of saintly and heroic men" (IR, 10). The Cistercians would succeed precisely because they did not jettison this insight of Benedict.

Probably the most famous monastery that was founded before Cîteaux was the abbey of Cluny in 910 in the Burgundy region of France. Cluny began as an attempt to return to a more primitive approach to living the Benedictine Rule. No one really planned for the abbey at Cluny to be a center of church reform, but for various reasons it turned into one. The popes and feudal leaders of the time often invited the abbots of Cluny to found new houses and to reform old ones.

As time went on, the Cluniacs became involved in more than internal monastic reform. They were called upon to intervene in some political matters as well. Most notable was their involvement in the "investiture controversy." The Cluniacs engaged in much diplomacy on this matter, but they were sometimes corrupted by the process. By the twelfth century, the Cluniac movement was being torn by both internal conflicts (largely brought about by its rapid expansion), and by external conflicts such as the investiture struggle (NCE 3:967). The rise of the Cistercians and other reform movements eventually overshadowed the Cluniacs.

The Cistercian movement was founded by Robert of Molesme in 1098. Robert had been an abbot of a Cluniac monastery but left to found a community at Molesme, which he envisioned as a monastic community that would follow the ascetic standards of the desert. But Molesme itself quickly became so big and successful that Robert again became dissatisfied. He got permission for himself and a small group of companions to move to another isolated place where they could live the Benedictine Rule more strictly. The place was Cîteaux, which initially was known simply as the "New Monastery."

Robert and his companions wanted to live "an ascetic life in poverty and perfect solitude, providing for themselves, like the Apostles of Christ, through their own labor" (IR, 14). Cistercian monasteries did admit lay brothers, known as *conversi*, to assist the monks in their agricultural labors. Before long, a set of regulations was established that decreed that Cistercian houses were to be located in isolated places and that monks were never to leave the monastery. The implications of these provisions were considerable: they meant, and the regulations specifically stated, that the monks were not to be involved in pastoral ministry.

The whole experiment nearly fell apart in 1099 when the monks of Molesme appealed to the pope to call Robert to return there as abbot. When he was ordered to do so by the pope's representative, he obeyed, bringing some of the monks of the New Monastery back with him. Nevertheless, Cîteaux survived. A new abbot, Alberic, was elected, who was succeeded by Stephen Harding in 1109. It was during Stephen Harding's tenure as abbot that Bernard entered the picture.

The Life of St. Bernard

As is the case for many historical figures who have become saints, it is sometimes difficult to separate the historical person from the cult figure who later developed. This is particularly true in the case of Bernard. The great Bernard scholar Adriaan Bredero has shown how the earliest biographies of Bernard were written largely to promote the cause of his canonization. Thus, his positive achievements were emphasized and his faults minimized. However, it is clear that Bernard was not a shining light in every aspect of his life, and indeed some historians have severely criticized Bernard for being harsh to his monks, abusive and unfair to his theological opponents, and manipulative in politics, among other things.

Are these accusations fair? The truth seems to be that Bernard can be categorized neither as a pure hero nor as a pure villain. Like many great people in history, he was a complex individual who had both strengths and weaknesses. One thing that can certainly be said about Bernard is that he was not lukewarm. A remark by Jean Leclercq, perhaps the foremost Bernard scholar of the twentieth century, is relevant here:

> If St. Bernard is a man before whom one must take a stand, it is because he embodies the very opposite of mediocrity. He is extraordinarily endowed by God and nothing that he does is ordinary. He excels in the most diverse areas, sometimes in areas that are positively opposed. (CS, 10)

Bernard was born in 1090 in Fontaines-lès-Dijon in Burgundy, France. He was one of seven children, with five brothers and one sister, all of whom were destined for a religious vocation. While his first biographer, William of St. Thierry, probably exaggerated Bernard's religiosity as a youth, it is safe to assume that Bernard was a pious child who took his faith very seriously. William reports that Bernard left the world in order to avoid the temptations of the flesh and to seek perfection.

It was not enough, however, that Bernard joined the monastery himself. He brought a large group of others with him, including several members of his own family. When Bernard had spoken publicly to convince others to come with him to Cîteaux, he was reportedly so persuasive that women clung to their husbands and sons to prevent them from going to hear him.

And so, in 1113, at the tender age of twenty-three, Bernard and thirty other men entered the monastery at Cîteaux. His plan was to live apart from the world, but things didn't work out quite this way. It has been estimated that Bernard ended up spending about one-third of his time as a monk away from the monastery. William of St. Thierry speaks of a major tension in Bernard's life, "a conflict in his heart between his great desire for souls and the desire to remain hidden from the attention of the world" (VP, 45).

Be that as it may, we can be sure that Bernard entered the monastery for the same reason that monks had done so for centuries: to come to know and to draw closer to God. He was, by all accounts, an exemplary monk, who engaged in mortifications, ate and drank little, and constantly immersed himself in the scriptures and the ancient commentaries of the fathers. This last activity, as we shall see, was abundantly reflected in his writings, which literally are brimming over with references to the scriptures.

In 1115, just a few years after he entered Cîteaux, Bernard was appointed the abbot of a new monastery in Clairvaux. William of St. Thierry describes life in Clairvaux as simple and ascetic; he remarks that it was a miracle that anyone could survive on the bread served there. Regarding Bernard's leadership, William concedes that at times Bernard expected too much of the monks and that he could be judgmental. At the same time, Bernard is said to have learned from his brother monks, and his dealings with them "grew in wisdom and understanding" (VP, 50). There is a famous story about a time when Bernard recognized he had been too harsh with one of the brothers, who happened to be his sibling Bartholomew. In a letter he wrote to another abbot, advising him to be merciful to a wayward monk, Bernard said:

One day he [Bartholomew] displeased me. Trembling with rage and using a threatening expression and tone of voice, I ordered him to leave the monastery. He immediately walked out, went to one of our barns, and stayed there. When I learned of this I wanted to call him back, but he stated his conditions: he would only return if he were received in his own rank; not in the last rank and as a fugitive, but as if he had been sent away lightly and without just cause. He maintained that he should not have to submit to due process of the Rule for his return, since proper procedures had not been observed in his dismissal. Distrusting my own judgment of this response and of my own actions, and because of the ties of blood between him and me, I entrusted the decision of this affair to the hands of all the brethren. Thus they judged, in my absence, that his return should not be subject to the letter of the Rule since it was certain that his dismissal had not been conducted in a regular fashion. (Letter 70, CS 41–42)

This letter shows us that Bernard himself matured in the qualities of humility and mercy that he tried to nurture in his brother monks. His modern biographers generally agree that, as time went on, Bernard became less severe and more compassionate.

It seems that the person with whom Bernard was most harsh was himself. By all accounts, he did not attend well to his own health, which was always fragile. Bernard had some kind of stomach disorder, probably an ulcer, which was made worse by his mortifications. At one point, the bishop put him under obedience to take a year of rest; when the year was up, Bernard went right back to his old ways. William of St. Thierry comments that although he did not look after himself very well, "for others he was full of tenderness and care" (VP, 62).

Bernard's charisma and leadership abilities led to his being asked to get involved in issues that would take him out of the monastery. The issues were both political and theological, and there is no need to recount all of them here. It will suffice to discuss three of them: Bernard's intervention in the disputed election of Pope Innocent II, his role in the condemnation of the theologian Peter Abelard, and his preaching of the ill-fated Second Crusade. Before we do this, a few preliminary remarks are in order.

It is hard to judge the extent to which Bernard may have enjoyed being in the public eye. In many of his letters, Bernard lamented his absence from the monastery. He once wrote to the monks at Clairvaux:

If my absence is irksome to you, you can be sure it is much more so to me. You are suffering from the absence of one person, but I am suffering from the absence of each and all of you, and this is something quite different and much more hard to bear. . . . It is not only that I am obliged, for the time being, to live away from you, when even to be king would be but a sorry servitude without you; but also because I am forced to move in affairs that trouble the peace of my soul, and are not perhaps very compatible with my vocation. (LB 144)

Notice that Bernard was well aware of the incongruity of a monk being involved in public affairs. In another letter, written to a Carthusian prior, he referred to himself as

a sort of modern chimaera, neither cleric nor layman. I have kept the habit of a monk, but I have long ago abandoned the life. I do not wish to tell you what I dare say you have heard from others: what I am doing, what are my purposes, through what dangers I pass in the world, or rather down what precipices I am hurled. If you have not heard, enquire and then, according to what you hear, give your advice and the support of your prayers. (LB 326)

A chimaera was a mythical beast, a mixture of a lion, goat, and dragon. Bernard certainly did not mean this statement as a compliment to himself; on the contrary, it suggests a certain measure of disappointment with the way his life unfolded.

There is no reason to doubt the sincerity of such statements as these, although one may be permitted to wonder if to some extent Bernard protested too much. He certainly entered with gusto into any situation where his intervention was requested, but he repeatedly insisted that he was only getting involved because he was pressed into service by the leaders of the church. I think it is safe to say that Bernard *would* have preferred to remain in the monastery but that on some level he was also energized by these outside involvements and the influence he was able to exert in situations such as the ones we are about to examine.

The first of these events took place beginning in 1130 with the death of Pope Honorius II. At the time, there was tremendous rivalry in the city of Rome between two powerful families, one of which had a papal candidate waiting in the wings, the cardinal priest Peter Pierleone. When Honorius was close to death it became clear that Peter was preparing to move into the position, and steps were taken to ensure a proper election so as to prevent him from usurping the office. But then Peter's rivals, led by the chancellor, Cardinal Haimeric, met quickly after Honorius's death and elected Gregory Papareschi pope, who took the name of Innocent II.

Suffice it to say that there was much that was irregular about the election. For example, there was a law that said no election of a new pontiff could be held until three days after a pope's death, which Haimeric and his supporters clearly violated. So an improper election was held after all. The Pierleone party promptly declared the election invalid and held another one, which resulted in the election of Peter, who took the name of Anacletus.

By this time, Bernard had already developed a strong reputation for resolving church conflicts, so he was called to get involved in the crisis. He threw his support behind Innocent and traveled extensively for several years defending his cause throughout Europe. But his support of Innocent has often been questioned. In Bernard's defense, some authors have pointed out that Innocent was simply the better candidate. It does seem to be true that Peter (Anacletus) had a bad reputation and Gregory (Innocent) had a very good one. Other authors have criticized Bernard, claiming that he backed Innocent because he was the candidate of choice of his good friend Cardinal Haimeric. Haimeric had been a friend of Bernard for quite some time and was an advocate of the kind of reform in the church that the Cistercians were promoting (LW, 133–34).

The second incident we will consider is Bernard's involvement in the case of an abbot named Peter Abelard. Abelard was a brilliant thinker, who pioneered a more logic-based approach to theology. For example, he wrote a text called *Sic et Non*, in which he juxtaposed contradictory texts from the Christian tradition and tried to resolve them through the use of reason. Bernard was not opposed to logic as such, but he firmly believed in the principle of "faith seeking understanding"—in other words, we believe *first* and then we show the reasonableness of our belief. Abelard, on the other hand, was willing to entertain the notion that understanding must precede faith. In his work *Historia Calamitatum* (The Story of Adversities), he described his early teaching in the area of theology:

> As chance would have it I first gave myself to discuss the foundation of our faith by analogies from reason, and composed for my students a theological tractate, *On the Unity and Trinity of God*. They had kept asking of me rational and philosophical expositions and insisting on what could be understood and not mere declarations, saying that a flow of words is useless if reason does not follow them, that nothing is believed unless it first be understood and that it is ridiculous for a man to proclaim to others what neither he

nor his pupils can grasp by their intelligence. Such a man, they said, was branded by the Lord as a blind leader of the blind. (HC, 43)

It was the kind of approach that many people in our own day would favor: "Give us a good argument, and then we will believe."

In 1139 William of St. Thierry wrote to Bernard about Abelard, pointing out the errors of some of his ideas. Bernard was concerned enough to meet with William and then with Abelard himself. Convinced now of the danger of Abelard's ideas, he wrote a *Treatise against the Errors of Abelard*, which he addressed to the pope. In the following year, Abelard challenged Bernard to a debate, to be held during a convocation of bishops in the city of Sens. However, the night before the debate was to take place, Bernard instigated a meeting with the bishops, where they prepared a list of erroneous propositions that they would use to accuse Abelard. The next day, Bernard opened the proceedings by reading these accusations aloud and then giving Abelard the chance to defend himself. What was supposed to be a debate turned into a trial. Abelard, quite understandably, refused to respond and appealed to Rome. But Bernard anticipated even this and had already sent letters calling for his condemnation, which did follow. Abelard was at Cluny when he received word of this. Through the kindness and generosity of the abbot there, he was offered a place to stay. There he remained until his death. It should be noted that he and Bernard were eventually reconciled.

It is not necessary to enter into the theological details of this controversy, but let us note that there was right and wrong on both sides. Abelard certainly provoked Bernard in calling for a debate, but Bernard was clearly underhanded in his tactics to have Abelard condemned. Abelard did not intend to be heretical, but he wanted only to use the tools of dialectic (logic) to defend the church against its opponents. In fact, Abelard's approach would later become a commonplace in the medieval universities and would be used in a more refined form by such great thinkers as St. Thomas Aquinas. On the other hand, Bernard was not anti-intellectual, but he understood theology from a tradition-ally Benedictine perspective. For Bernard as for his monastic forebears, the purpose of all learning, and indeed all reading of the Bible, was to draw one closer to God. Thus Bernard characterized his own purpose in expounding the scriptures as "not so much to explain words as to move hearts" (SC 16.1).

The final situation we will consider is Bernard's preaching of the Second Crusade, an attempt to free the Holy Land from the dominance of the Turks. This took place in 1146, at the request of Pope Eugenius III, who had been a monk in Clairvaux. We will have more to say in a later chapter about how Bernard responded to one of his own "sons" being appointed to the highest office in the church. For now, let us just note that Bernard preached the crusade with great fervor, declaring it blessed by God. In calling Christians to join the crusade, he appealed to them to make it like a pilgrimage, an opportunity to show their love for God. Although Bernard did not believe that the "infidels" should be forced to convert, he did believe it was necessary to contain them by force and so restore safety and order to the holy places.

The crusade, however, was a complete and utter failure, and it turned the tide of public opinion against Bernard. He spent his last years under a cloud of disapproval. In his work *On Consideration* he reflects at some length on this humiliation. He refuses to blame God, whose judgments, he recalls from Psalm 28, are always true. He ponders whether the defeat came because of infidelity and sin. He concludes that he would rather see himself blamed than God:

It means nothing to me to be judged by those who call good evil and evil good, who substitute light for darkness and darkness for light. I prefer that the murmuring of men be against us rather than against God, if a choice must be made. What an honor for me if he deigns to use me for a shield. Willingly I draw to myself the scurrilous tongues of detractors and the poisoned darts of blasphemers so that they do not reach him. I do not refuse to be stripped of glory to prevent an attack on the glory of God. (DC 2.4)

But notice how even in accepting this humiliation, Bernard hurls barbs at his detractors.

In none of these three situations does Bernard come out smelling like a rose. There can be little doubt that at times Bernard fell victim to narrow-mindedness, the arrogance of power, and the tendency to judge others unfairly. In the case of the crusade, we can question his promotion of violence against people he saw as enemies of the faith, and ask whether his response to the defeat was as humble as it could have been.

In the end, we are left with a complex and ambiguous picture of the abbot of Clairvaux. Catholics honor him as a saint, which is not to say that he did not have human faults and weaknesses, but that through God's grace he ultimately succeeded in being a shining example of the love of God and neighbor. This was the goal Bernard set for himself. In his best moments, he achieved it, and has helped countless other Christians throughout the ages to do the same.

An Introduction to Bernard's Writings

Bernard spoke and wrote with great eloquence on theological and spiritual matters. In fact, William notes that he sometimes spoke over the monks' heads—a fact that any modern reader of Bernard can readily appreciate! It is mainly because of his writings that Bernard has been remembered down through the ages. It is here that we encounter the "best of Bernard," his sublime insights on the Christian life. Although he was not a university-trained scholar, in his own way he was a theologian of the highest order, a person who always maintained the connection between theology and the human experience of the sacred.

The remainder of this book will focus on the written treasures that Bernard has bequeathed to us. In a way it is unfortunate that we will be reading Bernard in translation. Bernard's Latin prose has often been described as poetic, with turns of phrase, rhymes, and alliterations that simply cannot be duplicated in English or in other modern languages. To give just one example, in his twenty-third sermon on the Song of Songs, Bernard speaks about experiencing mystical union with God, which he describes in terms of entering a bridal chamber. He exclaims, "rara hora et parva mora!" In the English translation that I am using for this book, this phrase is rendered "How rare the time, and how short the stay!" (SC 23.15). Even one who does not read Latin can see how this rendition fails to capture the almost musical quality of the original text. Still, for all their inadequacies, translations of Bernard's works provide us with a window into his world for which we can be grateful.

It has already been mentioned that Bernard's writings are literally overflowing with references to the Bible. Bernard's theology is deeply biblical, but it will also strike the modern reader that Bernard uses the Bible in peculiar ways, particularly in his *Sermons on the Song of Songs*. He will often make connections that seem far-fetched by any stretch of the imagination. Bernard saw a great flexibility in interpreting biblical texts, as long as the literal or historical meaning was recognized and respected. He was deeply convinced that the Bible related directly to personal and communal spiritual experience, so perhaps we can forgive him for getting carried away at times with unlikely analogies. If there is anything that Christians need to hear today, it is that the Bible is immensely relevant to their personal and social lives. Writing many centuries before our own, Bernard still teaches this lesson to his modern readers. It is easy to see how he deserves the title Doctor of the Church, an honor bestowed on him by Pope Pius VIII in 1830.

In his writings, Bernard both promoted and exemplified a deep intimacy with God. This kind of experience is often called mystical. This word does not have to refer to extraordinary phenomena such as visions, ecstasies, and out-of-body experiences, though Bernard himself seems to have had some of these. Bernard wrote much that is relevant to practical, everyday Christian spirituality, and these are the texts that we will focus on in this book.

Unfortunately there is much that cannot be included. I am not sure that it is even possible to get Bernard scholars to agree on what writings are essential. It is my hope that this book will serve as a primer and lead the reader to further exploration of the writings of Bernard. In particular, there is much to be gained from reading in their entirety some of the works that we can only discuss in abbreviated form here.

Chapter 2

Divine Grace
and Human Freedom

There are few words that resonate more deeply for people in western culture today than the word "freedom." Many have lost their lives defending it or trying to win it. Young and old alike insist on their right to be free. In American culture in particular, freedom is sometimes hailed as the ultimate value. But what is freedom, and what does it mean to be free? This question has been pondered for centuries by countless thinkers. One of them was Bernard of Clairvaux.

Around 1128, Bernard wrote a theological treatise called *De gratia et libero arbitrio* (On Grace and Free Choice). It is more "dogmatic" in character than many of the other writings we will be considering in that it focuses on the basic *truths* that Christianity teaches about the relationship between God and human beings rather than on our personal *experience* of that relationship. But Bernard's more well-known spiritual works are built on the doctrinal foundation that he presents in *De gratia*, and there is much in this treatise that can help us to sort out contemporary questions about freedom. So let us begin our survey of Bernard texts here.

It would be no exaggeration to say that the issue Bernard raises in this treatise has been central to Christianity from the beginning. In the New Testament, it is most clearly expressed in the letter of Paul to the Romans, and Bernard refers to this letter frequently throughout the work. Bernard and his contemporaries understood Romans to teach that the sin of Adam enslaved the human race, Jew and Gentile alike, and we need the power (grace) of Christ to be saved. In other words, we cannot save ourselves. To use an analogy that Bernard uses, by our sin we have fallen into a hole that is so deep that we cannot get out by our own effort (DG 7.23).

Before going any further, we would do well to say a little more about the word "grace." For our purposes, it can be defined as God's activity or power in our lives. Christian theology has historically emphasized that God's most important activities in relation to human beings are three: creation, redemption, and the bestowing of eternal life. Bernard echoes this threefold emphasis in his treatise. Grace, however, can also refer to the active presence of God in each and every moment of our lives. God is the one in whom "we live and move and have our being" (Acts 17:28). Without God's sustaining presence, we cannot even breathe or think, let alone accomplish anything. We will find Bernard speaking of grace in this way as well.

Over the centuries, Paul's teaching in Romans came to be interpreted as follows: salvation is totally a gift of God, not our own doing. Even our movement to repent of our sins is a gift of God's Holy Spirit. In other words, even our seeking God's grace is itself an effect of God's grace. The question arose, however, whether this implies that God "does it all," and the human being literally does nothing and is just a totally passive recipient of grace. Is there no role at all for human freedom, that is, a free and voluntary response to God?

Some thinkers have in fact spoken of a "bondage of the will" and have wanted nothing to do with the idea that human beings "cooperate" in any way with God's grace. This approach was classically taken by some of the Protestant Reformers. But most theologians, including Bernard, have wanted to affirm some kind of genuine human freedom. His treatment of this issue draws on previous thinkers, such as St. Augustine, but is in many respects quite original.

Bernard begins his treatise with a recollection of a conversation he once had:

Once, in conversation, I happened to refer to my experience of God's grace, how I recognized myself as being impelled to good by its prevenient action, felt myself being borne along by it, and helped, with its help, to find perfection. "What part do *you* play, then," asked a bystander, "or what reward or prize do you hope for, if it is all God's work?" "What do you think yourself?" I replied. "Glorify God," said he, "who freely went before you, aroused and set you moving; and then live a worthy life to prove your gratitude for kindnesses received and your suitability for receiving more." (DG 1.1)

Here Bernard very cleverly prepares us for his argument by giving us one that he finds inadequate: that is, the idea that we only need grace to "get us started," so to say, in living an upright life, and the rest is up to us. In his opening lines, Bernard has already made it clear that this is not his perspective. He sees grace as carrying us every step of the way. At the same time, he recognizes a kernel of truth in the bystander's question. There *is* a part that human beings play in their own salvation. That part is what Bernard is going to call "free choice." He takes the liberty of rephrasing the question and then reaffirms his point:

Maybe you are saying, "What part, then, does free choice play?" I shall answer you in one word: it is saved. Take away free choice and there is nothing to be saved. Take away grace and there is no means of saving. Without the two combined, this work cannot be done: the one as operative principle, the other as object toward which, or in which, it is accomplished. God is the author of salvation, the free willing faculty merely capable of receiving it. None but God can give it, nothing but free choice receive it. What, therefore, is given by God alone and to free choice alone, can no more happen without the recipient's consent than without the bestower's grace. Consequently, free choice is said to co-operate with operating grace in its act of consent, or in other words, in its process of being saved. For, to consent is to be saved. (DG 1.2)

Pay careful attention to the nuances of Bernard's language here. Bernard does not mean to imply that our consent is a kind of permission that we give God to save us. The role of consent is rather to *receive* the gift of salvation. Thus, while it is we who give the consent (and in this sense we can be said to "co-operate" with God's grace), it is God who brings it about that we consent (i.e., God is wholly the author of salvation). To put it in another way, salvation comes about not *by* but *with* our consent.

For Bernard, free choice is what constitutes fundamental human freedom. Bernard goes on to assert that because of its innate freedom, the human will "can be compelled by no force or necessity to dissent from itself, or to consent in any matter in spite of itself" (DG 3.6). In other words, our will is its own master. Bernard would see exceptions in the case of infants and the "mentally deficient" (DG 2.5).

But the will's freedom from external coercion does not, for Bernard, constitute the fullness of freedom. He goes on to present a fairly nuanced understanding of the scope and limits of free choice.

Three Levels of Freedom

Moving now into the main part of his argument, Bernard asserts:

Free though it is, [free choice] does not signify the freedom of which the Apostle [Paul] says: "Where the Spirit of the Lord is, there is freedom." [2 Corinthians 3:17] For here he means freedom from sin, as he points out elsewhere: "When you were slaves of sin, you were free in regard to righteousness. But now that you have been set free from sin and have become slaves of God, the return you get is sanctification and its end, eternal life." [Romans 6:20, 22] (DG 3.6)

Notice, first, the close spacing of the two scripture quotations in this passage. This is typical of Bernard's writings. In some Bernard texts, including parts of this treatise, scripture references are found on almost every line.

This statement introduces the heart of Bernard's argument: freedom, in its fullest sense, is more than just being free from external coercion; it includes freedom from sin in this life and freedom from the destruction of our bodies in death, that is, the ability to enter into heavenly glory, which Bernard sees as ultimately involving both body and soul. Negatively, Bernard describes these freedoms with the terms freedom from necessity (=free choice), freedom from sin, and freedom from sorrow. Positively, he calls them freedom of nature, freedom of grace, and freedom of life or glory. Notice how Bernard's analysis here follows the threefold understanding of grace described at the beginning of this chapter:

For in the first place, we were created with free will and willing freedom, a creature noble in God's eyes. Secondly, we are re-formed in innocence, a new creature in Christ: and thirdly, we are raised up to glory, a perfect creature in the Spirit. The first freedom is thus a title of considerable honor; the second, of even greater power; and the last, of total happiness. By the first, we have the advantage over other living things; by the second, over the flesh; while by the third, we cast down death itself. (DG 3:7)

The question lurking behind this analysis, of course, is whether and how human beings can enjoy all three freedoms. Bernard will argue that Jesus possesses all three freedoms in their fullness. Adam and Eve possessed all of them—though in a different way than Jesus, as we shall see—until they sinned. Sin put limits on the first freedom (free choice) and deprived human beings of the other two. The saving grace of Christ won them back.

It is important to review exactly how Bernard understands free choice. It can do no more than to "aim our desire" (DG 4.10) at good or evil. It cannot empower us to *do* the good; this power is rooted in the second freedom, freedom from sin. Note carefully the way Bernard develops this point:

Even freedom of choice is to some extent held captive as long as it is unaccompanied or imperfectly accompanied by the two remaining freedoms; . . . To will lies in our power indeed as a result of free choice, but not to carry out what we will. I am not saying to will the good or to will the bad, but simply to will. For to will the good indicates an achievement; and to will the bad, a defect; whereas simply to will denotes the subject itself, which does either the achieving or the failing. To this subject, however, creating grace gives existence. Saving grace gives it the achievement. But when it fails, it is to blame for its own failure. Free choice, accordingly, constitutes us willers; grace, willers of the good. (DG 6.16)

What Bernard really means here, although he does not say it in so many words, is that after the sin of Adam and Eve, the only choices that human beings can both *will* and *carry out*, apart from saving grace, are indifferent or evil ones. Freedom of choice has not been taken away, but its scope has now been limited.

It is significant that Bernard inserts a statement about the "willing subject," that is, the human person. He reminds us that creating grace gives the willing subject its *very existence*. For the believing Christian, any discussion of freedom must begin with the recognition that our very life is a gift from God. As Paul puts it in 1 Corinthians 6:17: "Do you not know that your body is a temple of the Holy Spirit within you, which you have from God, and that you are not your own?"

Yet Bernard will say that there *is* a sense in which we are "our own." He states, "free will makes us our own; bad will, the devil's; and good will, God's" (DG 6.18). It is important to Bernard that we can claim free choice as something we *possess* by our very nature as human beings. But because of sin, we do not possess it in its perfect form:

Whether we belong to God or the devil, this does not prevent us from being also our own. For on either side freedom of choice continues to operate, and so the ground of merit remains, inasmuch as, when we are bad we are rightly punished, since we have become so of our own free choice, or when we are good we are glorified, since we could not have become so without a similar decision of our will. It is our own will that enslaves us to the devil, not his power; whereas, God's grace subjects us to God, not our will. Our will, created good (as must be granted) by the good God, shall nevertheless be perfect only when perfectly subjected to its Creator. (DG 6.18)

Thus, free choice, a gift of creating grace, *remains* in sinful human beings, but it is now imperfect. According to Bernard, this is the dilemma that Paul refers to in Romans 7:18 when he says, "'I can will what is right, but I cannot do it.' He realized that to will was possible to him as a result of free choice, but that for this will to be perfect he stood in need of [saving] grace" (DG 6.18).

The Consequences of Sin

Bernard next deals with the question: didn't Adam and Eve possess the three freedoms? If so, how could they have lost them? Bernard reasserts his axiom that free choice, in and of itself, cannot be lost under any circumstances. Adam and Eve initially possessed the other two freedoms as well, but they lost them through sin. How is this possible? If Adam and Eve were created free from sin, why did they not remain so?

In answering this question, Bernard uses a form of argument that is similar to the more rational approach taken by Abelard and later thinkers like Thomas Aquinas: he makes a logical distinction. Borrowing from Augustine, Bernard argues that freedom from sin and freedom from sorrow each admit of two degrees. He expresses the difference by the simple inversion of two Latin words. The higher freedom from sin consists in not being able to sin (*non posse peccare*), while the lower consists in being able not to sin (*posse non peccare*). Similarly, the higher freedom from sorrow consists in not being able to be disturbed (*non posse turbari*), while the lower consists in being able not to be disturbed (*posse non turbari*).

Thus, man received in his very nature, along with full freedom of choice, the lower degree of each of these freedoms; and when he sinned, he fell from both. In losing completely his freedom of counsel, he fell from not being able to sin to not being able not to sin. Likewise, from being able not to be disturbed, he fell to not being able not to be disturbed, with the total loss of his freedom of pleasure. There only remained, for his punishment, the freedom of choice through which he lost the others; that he could not lose. (DG 7.21)

It might be easier to think of the situation after sin in these terms: we maintain our free choice, but now we are *only* able to sin and *only* able to be disturbed or sorrowful. In other words, we are subject to sin and death, but Jesus, as mentioned earlier, possesses all three freedoms in their fullness.

This leads to the question: if Jesus was free from sorrow, why did he have to experience death on the cross? Bernard's answer is simple: Jesus freely chose to do this for our salvation:

No one took away his life from him, but he laid it down of his own accord. In a word, as the Prophet [Isaiah] had foretold, "He was offered up because he willed it" [see Isaiah 53:7] and even as, at the time of his own choosing, he was "born of a woman, born under the law, to redeem those who were under the law" [Galatians 4:4f]. Hence he, too, was subject to the law of suffering; but this was because he willed to be, in order that, himself free among sufferers and sinners, he might lift from his brothers' [and sisters'] shoulders the yoke of both sin and suffering. (DG 3.8)

This certainly comes as good news, but one might be tempted to ask further: why didn't God create us so that we would not have been able to sin to begin with? It is almost as if Bernard anticipates this question, for he goes on to say:

Among all living beings, to man alone was given the ability to sin, as part of his prerogative of free choice. But he was given it, not that he might, but rather that he might appear the more glorious did he not sin when he was capable of doing so. . . . No failure this of the bestower, but rather of the abuser, who made over to the service of sin that faculty he had received for the glory of not sinning. For, though the root of his sin lay in the ability received, yet he sinned, not because he was able to, but because he willed to. (DG 7:22)

At this point we should pause and consider the implications of what Bernard has said here. At the beginning of the chapter it was noted how important freedom of choice is for people today. Would we prefer not to have this freedom? I suspect not. Obviously, God thinks freedom of choice is important too. Human beings were created to be like God in a unique sense; thus Bernard will see in free choice the essence of our being made "in God's image." God certainly took a risk in creating free beings, but the alternative would have been the absence of creatures who could relate to God consciously and willingly.

Bernard says that it would have been to our credit that we were able to sin and yet did not choose to do so. But in fact, human beings went on to abuse their freedom. Bernard does not seem to think that this was inevitable. Remember, he just said that we sinned not because we were *able* to but because we *wanted* to. Once the offense was committed, however, we lost the freedoms from sin and sorrow. From this point on, we were able *only* to sin, because our will could not repair the damage it had done to itself:

If [the sinner] fell by the power of his will, this does not mean that he was equally free to rise again by that same power. The ability to remain standing lest he fall was indeed given to his will, but not to get up again once he fell. It is not as easy to climb out of a pit as to fall into one. By his will alone, man fell into the pit of sin; but he cannot climb out of his will alone, since now, even if he wishes he cannot not sin. (DG 7.23)

Bernard insists that this state of affairs does not obliterate free choice:

Free choice, consequently, still remains, even after man's sin, tinged with sorrow but intact. And the fact that he can in no way extricate himself either from sin or sorrow signifies, not the destruction of free choice, but the privation of the other two freedoms. . . . If he finds himself unable simply to will the good, this is a sign that he lacks free counsel, not free choice. And if he finds himself powerless, not indeed to will the good, but to accomplish that good which he already wills, let him recognize that it is not free choice that is wanting to him, but free pleasure. (DG 8.24)

Bernard says here that free choice is "tinged with sorrow but intact." The loss of the other two freedoms, however, has clearly limited its potential. Bernard goes on to say that although free choice "always carries on unimpaired," it does not of itself have the power to lift us out of our sinful condition. If, prior to sin, free choice was unable to advance us to the higher levels of the other freedoms, whereby we would not be able to sin or be disturbed, "how much less chance does it stand, now that it is deprived of them, of raising itself up by its own power from evil to that former level which was good" (DG 8.25).

The Restoration of Freedom

In Romans 7:24, having stated that because of sin he is not able to carry out the good that he wants to do, Paul exclaims, "Who will rescue me from this body of death? Thanks be to God through Jesus Christ our Lord!" This is of course the solution to which Bernard has been leading us. Free choice is powerless to restore to us the other freedoms that were lost through sin:

And this is where Christ comes in. In him, man possesses the necessary "power of God and the wisdom of God" [1 Corinthians 1:24], who, inasmuch as he is wisdom, pours back into man true wisdom, and so restores to him his free counsel; and inasmuch as he is power, renews his full power, and so restores to him his free pleasure. (DG 8.26)

Bernard goes on to say that the perfection of these things must wait until the next life. In our present existence, we cannot be totally rid of sin and sorrow. When we let the grace of God take over in our lives, "we are repairing the image of God in us, and the way is being paved, by grace, for the retrieving of that former honor which we forfeited by sin" (DG 8.27).

At this point, Bernard diverts his attention to the thesis that free choice constitutes the essence of our being made in the image of God, and the other two freedoms represent our likeness to God. We are going to skip over this discussion. It is not essential to the argument, and frankly, Bernard is not consistent here with what he says in other works.

Bernard's next step is to assert that neither the grace of God, on the one hand, nor temptation, on the other, takes anything away from free choice. Starting with grace,

Bernard is emphatic that salvation does not come about apart from our consent:

The creator endowed his rational creature, as we have said, with this prerogative of his divine dignity: that even as he himself was independent and master of his own will and hence not good by any necessity, so the creature, too, was made his own master to that extent that he would become evil only by his will and so justly be damned, or remain good by his will and deservedly be saved. Not that his will alone would be capable of gaining him salvation, but would never stand a chance of gaining it without his will. *No one is unwillingly saved.* (DG 11.36, emphasis added)

Note again that Bernard wants to assert two things about free choice in the person who is redeemed. It is God's grace, which comes to us through Christ, that turns the will to the good; but our consent is a part of this process. Bernard insists that in changing the will of sinful human beings, God "does not take away their freedom, but transfers its allegiance" (DG 11.36).

Bernard now moves to the question of temptation. He quotes Romans 7:23 as follows: "I find in my members another law at war with the law of my mind and making me captive to the law of sin which dwells in my members" (DG 11.37). Bernard contends that although scripture passages like this seem to deny free choice, nevertheless it remains intact. It is not freedom of choice that Paul is talking about here but rather freedom from sin.

Bernard even considers the question of those who are forced through fear to deny their faith. He uses Peter's denial of Jesus as his example. According to Bernard, Peter loved Christ and did not want to deny him, but more powerful than this love was his fear of death. It is not that he

didn't love Christ, it is that he loved himself too much.
Bernard concludes:

Had [Peter] not loved Christ, his denial would not have
been unwilling; but had he not loved himself even more,
there would not have been any denial. We must consequently grant that the man was forced, if not to change,
yet to dissemble his own will: forced, I say, not to recede
from the love of God, but somewhat to yield to love of
self. (DG 12.39)

Doesn't this mean that Peter's will was not free? No,
Bernard says; this would only be true if the will "could be
forced by some cause other than itself. If, however, it was
itself that did the forcing, being at once subjected and sub-
jecting, then, just when it seemed to lose its freedom, it
actually received it." The threat of punishment or death
does not negate freedom of choice but only shows the will
to be weak. "Its weakness is its own, its health not its own,
but from the Spirit of the Lord. And it is made healthy
when it is renewed" (DG 12.39).

Bernard summarizes his understanding of the will by
using an image, which at this point in the treatise comes as
a welcome relief from all the fine distinctions he has been
making:

Able to go in either direction, [the will] is, as it were, on
the sloping side of a fairly steep mountain. It is so weak-
ened by its desires by the flesh that only with the Spirit
constantly helping its infirmity through grace is it capable
of righteousness (which, to quote the Prophet [Psalm
36:6], is like the mountains of God), capable of ascend-
ing from strength to strength right up to the summit.
Without that help, borne by the pull of its own weight,
it would tumble headlong down the precipice, from vice
to vice. (DG 12.41)

What it all comes down to is this: we need the grace of God to be righteous. Without it, we are doomed to remain in sin.

God's Part and Our Part

There is one other issue that Bernard needs to deal with before he puts it all together: the question of merit. Recall the question that the bystander asked Bernard at the beginning of the treatise: "What reward or prize do you hope for, if it is all God's work?" Does our consent have any meritorious value in the eyes of God? Does it make us deserving of the reward of heaven? Bernard begins by reminding us:

Free choice must not seek the reason for its condemnation anywhere outside of itself, since its own fault alone condemns it; nor within itself the merit of its salvation, since mercy alone is responsible for saving it. Vain indeed, would be its efforts to do good were grace not at hand to help it; they would not even [exist], had they received no stimulus. (DG 13.42; I have changed "be" to "exist" because I think it expresses the sense of the Latin text better.)

Recall that a key element of traditional church teaching on salvation was that even our desire for grace is an effect of grace. This is what Bernard is paying homage to here.

Bernard talks about how God can operate through creatures without their consent, against their consent, or with their consent. The first case refers to animals and inanimate objects. Since they cannot act consciously and are incapable of consent, they cannot win merits. The second case refers to wicked angels and human beings. They dissent from the good and are therefore without merit; God can nevertheless accomplish good through them in spite of them.

The third case refers to angels and humans who consent

to God's will. Quoting Paul's statement in 1 Corinthians 3:9 that "we are God's fellow-workers," he states his belief that these will be rewarded for their good deeds. However, he understands this in the way that Augustine once put it: God chooses to crown as our merits what in fact are God's own gifts. In Bernard's words,

God, therefore, kindly gives man the credit, as often as he deigns to perform some good act through him and with him. That is why we presume to apply to ourselves the title of "God's fellow workers," co-operators with the Holy Spirit, meriters of the kingdom, in that we have become united with the divine will by our own voluntary consent. (DG 13.45).

So, we have come full circle. The "entire function and the sole merit of free choice lie in its consent" (DG 14.46). Bernard does not see himself as inventing this insight; he claims it is solidly rooted in the teaching of Paul:

These words are not mine but the Apostle's, who attributes to God and not to his own choosing power, everything susceptible of good: thinking, willing, and accomplishing for his good pleasure. If, then, God works these three things in us, namely thinking, willing, and accomplishing the good, the first he does without us; the second, with us; and the third, through us. (DG 14.46).

The reference is to Philippians 2:13, which Bernard modifies a bit; Paul does not actually mention "thinking," but only willing and working. This is a good example of the way in which Bernard feels free to bend a text to suit his purposes. In this case, at least, he does not stray *too* far from what the text actually says. The New Revised Standard Version of the Bible translates the passage as follows: "it is God who is at work in you, enabling you both to will and to work for his good pleasure."

Finally we come to the passage that I consider the most important one of the treatise. Here Bernard summarizes the part that God plays and the part that we play:

There can be no doubt, therefore, that the beginning of our salvation rests with God, and is enacted neither through us nor with us. The consent and the work, however, though not originating from us, nevertheless are not without us. . . . What was begun by grace alone, is completed by grace and free choice together, in such a way that they contribute to each new achievement not singly but jointly; not by turns, but simultaneously. It is not as if grace did one half of the work and free choice the other; but each does the whole work, according to its own peculiar contribution. Grace does the whole work, and so does free choice—with this one qualification: that whereas the whole is done *in* free choice, so is the whole done *of* grace. (DG 14.47)

This statement is a masterful and elegant expression of the relationship between divine grace and human freedom. Ultimately, everything depends on grace, and grace is the context in which even our response is enacted. While God does what is proper to God, however, we must do what is proper to us. God can no more do the consenting for us than we can do the motivating and the guiding for God. God must give one hundred percent and we must give one hundred percent, recognizing that our one hundred percent wouldn't even be possible without the gift of grace.

Bernard immediately follows this passage with the statement "We trust the reader may be pleased to find that we have never strayed far from the Apostle's meaning, and that wherever our words may wander, we find ourselves often returning to almost his very words" (DG 14.48). He then quotes Romans 9:16 on how everything depends on

God's mercy. While the treatise *On Grace and Free Choice* is not exactly a commentary on Paul's letter to the Romans, it is clear that Bernard's main goal is to resolve the issues raised in that letter.

Bernard wraps up his argument with a statement that recapitulates the notion of a threefold activity of grace:

Those, therefore, who are possessed of true wisdom, acknowledge a threefold operation, not indeed of free choice, but of divine grace in, or concerning, free choice. The first is creation; the second, reformation; and the third, consummation. Created first in Christ unto freedom of will, by the second we are reformed through Christ unto the spirit of freedom, lastly to reach fulfillment with Christ unto the state of eternity. (DG 14.49)

In other words, God creates us with the gift of free choice; God reforms or repairs free choice after we have damaged (but not destroyed) it by sin; and God brings our consent to fulfillment in heaven.

The Significance of Bernard's Treatise

For Bernard of Clairvaux, freedom in its *fullest* sense is not merely a lack of restraint or a license to do as one pleases. We indeed have "freedom from necessity," but paradoxically this kind of freedom, in and of itself, imprisons us by limiting the horizon of our choices to options that are or result in evil. The fullness of freedom only comes when our free choice cooperates with the gift of God's grace. God then transforms our free choice so that it can bear fruit in faithfulness, good works, and ultimately eternal life.

In our world today, there are many who would define freedom as mere "freedom from necessity," without recognizing that this so-called freedom ends up not being freedom at all. For example, those who see no boundaries to sexual expression quickly find themselves exploiting other human beings and doing serious psychological, spiritual, and sometimes even physical damage to others and to themselves. Those who see no boundaries to the consumption of alcohol and other addictive substances soon find themselves victimized as addicts, destroying their own health and well-being and often other people's in the process.

If Bernard were alive today, none of this would come as a surprise. To him, it is self-evident that apart from God's saving power, freedom from necessity will only lead us into trouble. True freedom comes from achieving our fullest potential as human beings, and this can only happen when we allow God to be our guide. As our creator, God knows what is best for us.

Throughout the treatise, Bernard periodically reminds his readers that, ultimately, we can do nothing without God: we cannot even exist or think, let alone accomplish anything. This corresponds to the understanding of grace as energizing and sustaining every moment of our lives, which was mentioned at the beginning of the chapter. Thus, at the beginning of the last chapter of *De gratia*, after reminding us that the function and merit of free choice lie in its consent, Bernard adds, "Not that this consent, in which all merit consists, is its own doing, since we are unable even to think anything of ourselves, which is less than to consent" (DG 14.46).

It is noteworthy that Paul himself sees freedom and slavery as being in a symbiotic relationship. When we are free from righteousness, we are slaves of sin; and when we are free from sin, we are slaves of righteousness (see Romans 6:17–20). In other words, for Paul there is really no such thing as freedom as such; it is either "freedom from" or "freedom for." Bernard makes essentially the same point in his treatise. Though he wants to hold on to the notion that free choice in and of itself deserves to be called freedom, he recognizes that full freedom only comes to us when we *surrender* ourselves to divine grace. Conversely, we severely limit our freedom when we surrender to sin.

There are certainly parts of Bernard's argument in this treatise with which one might take issue today. Paul's letter to the Romans is itself understood somewhat differently today than it was in Bernard's time, which leads to different accents of interpretation and new insights of which Bernard could not even conceive. But I would suggest that much of what Bernard says here remains valuable for our spiritual life. The question that Bernard basically raises for Christian believers is this: are we willing to let God direct our lives? If we answer yes, then Bernard says we will truly be free. That yes opens us up to the possibility of a conversion experience, which in turn leads us to a profound experience of the love of God and neighbor. It is to these central themes of Bernard's spiritual writings that we now turn.

Chapter 3

Conversion

"Reform your lives! The reign of God is at hand!" These words have been spoken over and over again in the history of Christianity, starting with Jesus himself (Mark 1:15). To be a Christian has always meant being willing to be converted (Latin, *convertere*, "to turn around"). Conversion is not a word that captures the popular imagination, like "freedom." Perhaps this is because people correctly link it with the painful process of self-examination and self-reformation—not the most appealing of topics. Yet people do have a sense that conversion is important. It is surely no accident that most churches are full every year on Ash Wednesday.

In the last chapter, we examined Bernard's belief in the genuine capacity of human beings to receive the gift of grace. Our consent begins the process of conversion, a process that Bernard believes needs to continue throughout our lifetime. At the outset we should acknowledge that Bernard has a strong bias when it comes to conversion. He really believes that it happens most effectively and completely in the monastery. In fact, much of his writing on conversion is addressed specifically to his monks and not to a more general audience.

It is nevertheless worthwhile to explore some of these

writings because they have a significance that transcends their monastic context. In this chapter, we will focus on Bernard's treatise *The Steps of Humility and Pride,* with some reference to his sermons on conversion and other texts.

The Steps of Humility and Pride was Bernard's first published work, and it has also been one of his most popular over the centuries. The treatise is based on the seventh chapter of the Rule of St. Benedict, in which Benedict outlines twelve steps of humility, which correspond to progress in conversion. The title of Bernard's treatise is actually a bit deceptive because Bernard speaks in detail only of the steps of pride, taking the opposite of Benedict's approach. After describing the descent from the highest humility to the depths of pride, Bernard abruptly ends his work. He remarks,

It looks as if I had described the steps of pride rather than those of humility. All I can say is that I can teach only what I know myself. I could not very well describe the way up because I am more used to falling down than to climbing. St. Benedict describes the steps of humility to you because he had them in his heart; I can only tell you what I know myself, the downward path. However, if you study this carefully you will find the way up. (GH 22.57)

What are we to make of this statement? In reviewing Bernard's life story, we have already seen that humility is not the first word that comes to mind to describe his personality. M. Basil Pennington remarks that "the man who wrote the *Steps of Humility* was not humble by origin, nature, or temperament. It was a virtue, he knew from experience, that had to be cultivated—and at a price" (GH, introduction, p. 7). It is appropriate to recall here that Bernard did become more humble over the years in dealing with his brother monks, and he certainly was well aware of his own shortcomings.

Then there is the question of Bernard's opposite arrangement of Benedict's material. In this commentary, I am going to follow Benedict's lead and speak of the way *up* the ladder of humility, using Bernard's treatise to illustrate the struggles that we face along the way. Bernard himself invites us to do this when he says, "if you study this carefully you will find the way up." So, in effect, we will be reading most of Bernard's treatise "backwards." I think this will leave the reader with a better understanding of Bernard's meaning, particularly when we apply his words to a broader context than the monastery.

The Goal of Humility: The Attainment of Truth

Before he gets to the specific steps of humility and pride, Bernard speaks at some length about what we will find when we get to the top of the steps: the truth. Humility itself is defined as a kind of truth; following the lead of St. Augustine, Bernard defines it as "a virtue by which a man has a low opinion of himself because he knows himself well" (GH 1.2). Elsewhere, Bernard is emphatic that humility must be based on the truth. In a letter to a new abbot who complained to Bernard that he was "new to the office and inexperienced," Bernard says,

Barren modesty is not acceptable nor is humility praiseworthy when it is not in accordance with the facts. Attend to your duty. Put aside false modesty by considering your position. . . . You say you have no capacity for these things. As though you would have to answer for what you cannot do as well as for what you can! No, prepare yourself to answer for the one talent entrusted to you, and set your mind easy about the rest. If you have received much, then give much; if little, then give little. (LB 259.2)

This remark makes it clear that Bernard does not wish to define humility in terms of false modesty, as it is sometimes defined in our own day. To be humble is to accept the truth about oneself; this means accepting our talents as well as facing up to our deficiencies.

According to Bernard, there are two other truths that accompany humility: love and contemplation. These three things are the "fruits" of climbing the steps of humility. Bernard sees them as three degrees of truth:

There are three degrees in the perception of truth. . . . We must look for truth in ourselves; in our neighbors; in itself. We look for truth in ourselves when we judge ourselves; in our neighbors when we have sympathy for their sufferings; in itself when we contemplate it with a clean heart. It is important to observe the order of these degrees as well as their number. First of all, truth teaches us that we must look for it in our neighbors before we seek it in itself. You will then see easily why you must seek it in yourself before you seek it in your neighbors. (GH 3.6)

Bernard is emphatic that truth is attained in the order that he has just described. First, we need to know ourselves for what we are. This is the truth of humility. Then, we need to know our neighbors, which we can only do by learning how to be compassionate toward them. This is the truth of love. Notice that Bernard generally uses love here not in the sense of romantic love or affection, but in the sense of charity, reaching out to others in their need and identifying with them. Bernard's expansion of this point is striking in its eloquence:

The merciful quickly grasp the truth in their neighbors when their heart goes out to them with a love that unites them so closely that they feel the neighbors' good and ill as if it were their own. With the weak they are weak, with the scandalized they are on fire. They "rejoice with those who rejoice and weep with those who weep." Their hearts are made more clear-sighted by love and they experience the delight of contemplating truth, not now in others but in itself, and for love of it they bear their neighbors' sorrows. A man who does not live in harmony with his brothers, who mocks at those who weep and sneers at those who are glad, has no sympathy with them because their feelings do not affect him, he can never really see the truth in others. . . . It is fellow-sufferers that readily feel compassion for the sick and the hungry. For just as pure truth is seen only by the pure of heart, so also a brother's miseries are truly experienced only by one who has misery in his own heart. You will never have real mercy for the failings of another until you know and realize that you have the same failings in your soul. (GH 3.6)

What Bernard describes here in relation to love of neighbor is what today is usually called "empathy." Empathy is more than sympathy because it implies that we have "been there," that we understand our neighbors' struggles because we have struggled ourselves, and recognize our own lowliness. Bernard is convinced that this experience will lead us to the third degree of truth, contemplation. This is where we gaze on truth itself. We will say more about this experience in the following two chapters.

The person who set the example for us in all of this is Jesus:

He willed to suffer so that he might know compassion; to learn mercy he shared our misery. It is written: "He learned obedience from the things he suffered" [Hebrews 5:8], and he learned mercy in the same way. I do not mean that he did not know how to be merciful before; his mercy is from eternity to eternity; but what in his divine nature he knows from all eternity he learned by experience in time. (GH 3.6)

Bernard launches into a long excursus at this point, in which he tries to explain the relationship between Jesus's divine and human knowledge. The details of this are not important for our purposes, but in this section he misquotes a passage of scripture and proceeds to build an argument based on the misunderstood passage. To his credit, Bernard later attaches a *retractio* (retraction) to the beginning of the treatise, where he apologizes for his error. In a treatise on humility, it is noteworthy that Bernard is willing to acknowledge his own mistakes.

Coming back to his subject, Bernard makes the point that if Christ submitted to human misery for our sake, so much more should we pay attention to our own misery and that of others (GH 4.13). If we persevere in these things, we will finally come to the third degree of truth, contemplation. Bernard summarizes:

These are the three steps of truth. We climb to the first by the toil of humility, to the second by a deep feeling of compassion, and to the third by the ecstasy of contemplation. On the first step we experience the severity of truth, on the second its tenderness, on the third its purity. Reason brings us to the first as we judge ourselves; compassion brings us to the second when we have mercy on others; on the third the purity of truth sweeps us up to the sight of things invisible. (GH 6.19)

Does all of this sound suspiciously trinitarian? Bernard goes on to suggest that the Son works in the first step by

THE TWELVE STEPS OF HUMILITY	THE TWELVE STEPS OF PRIDE

Relation to the Community

12. Always to show the humility in one's heart, in one's bearing, keeping the eyes lowered	1. Curiosity: when the eyes and the other senses attend to what is not one's concern
11. That the monk should speak few and reasonable words and with a moderate voice	2. Levity of mind, known by words that bespeak unreasonable joy and sadness
10. Not to be over-ready to laugh	3. Silly mirth, with over-much laughing
9. To keep silent until one is questioned	4. Boasting and too much talking
8. To keep to the common rule of the monastery	5. Singularity, proud esteem of one's own ways
7. To believe and admit that one is less than others	6. Self-assertion; believing one is holier than others

Relation to Superiors

6. To confess and to believe that one is unworthy and useless for anything	7. Presumption: meddling with everything
5. To confess one's sins	8. Defending one's sins
4. To hold fast to patience amidst hard and rough things for the sake of obedience	9. Hypocritical confession, which can be tested by harsh reproof
3. To submit to superiors in all obedience	10. Rebellion against superiors and brethren

Relation to God

2. Not to love one's own will	11. Freedom in sinning
1. In the fear of God to be constantly on the watch	12. The habit of sin
	(GH, table of contents)

giving us an example of humility; the Spirit works in the second step by giving us the gift of charity; and the Father works in the third step by receiving us into glory. However, Bernard hastens to add that

Truth is the proper title, not of the Son alone but of the Spirit and the Father too, so that it must be made quite clear, while giving full acknowledgement to the properties of Persons that it is the one Truth who works at all these stages: in the first teaching as a Master, in the second consoling as a Friend and Brother, in the third embracing as a Father. (GH 7.20)

Bernard concludes this section of the treatise by referring to St. Paul as one whom he thinks experienced the three degrees of truth (GH 8).

Remember that these degrees of truth are being presented as the *goal* of humility. Let us now look at the actual steps of humility that lead us to this goal, and to the steps of pride that lead us away from it. Bernard also sees these twelve steps in a threefold division. The chart on the next page lists the twelve steps and how they relate to each other:

Notice that there is a direct correlation between each step of humility and pride. Bernard sees the first two steps of humility and the last two steps of pride as taking place outside of the monastery. The other ten steps of each take place within the monastery. In this commentary, we will explore the significance of Bernard's remarks in terms of how they might apply not only to those who live a formal monastic life but to all Christian believers.

Before we review these steps of humility, let us recall a point that was made in the last chapter. Bernard thinks that all human goodness flows from God's grace. At the beginning of a sermon on conversion that he wrote for a group of clerics, Bernard says:

Indeed, the word of God is living and active and his voice is powerful and majestic. For he spoke and they were created. He said "let there be light" and there was light. He said "be converted" and the children of men were converted. *Clearly, then, the conversion of souls is the working of the divine, not the human, voice.* Simon, the son of John, was called and appointed a fisher of men by the Lord, and yet even he toiled all night in vain and took nothing until, letting down his nets at the Lord's word, he was able to enclose a great shoal. (CO 1.2, emphasis added)

Growth in holiness happens when we say yes to God's grace, consenting to this voice that calls us to conversion. Pride happens when we compromise that yes to varying degrees.

Humility before God

So, we begin with Benedict's first step of humility: in the fear of God to be constantly on the watch. Benedict expands on this point as follows:

[A person seeking humility] must *constantly* remember everything that God has commanded, keeping in mind that all who despise God will burn in hell for their sins, and all who fear God have everlasting life awaiting them. While he guards himself *at every moment* from sins and vices of thought or tongue, of hand or foot, of self-will or bodily desire, let him recall that he is *always* seen by God in heaven, that his actions *everywhere* are in God's sight and are reported by angels *at every hour.* (RB 7.10, emphasis added)

Notice here the frequent references to constancy. Humility begins with cultivating the habit of continuous awareness of God's presence and God's commandments.

In contrast to this person who constantly, at every moment, keeps God in mind, Bernard presents the person who is caught in the habit of sin. Once pleasure in sin has been experienced,

Sin is repeated and the pleasure grows. Old desires revive, conscience is dulled, habit tightens its grasp. . . . Good and evil mean nothing to [the sinner] now. He is ready to serve sin heart, hand, and foot with thoughts, acts, and plans unchecked. He seeks new ways of sinning. The plans of his heart, the ready words of his mouth, the works of his hands, are at the service of every impulse. (GH 21.51)

It is almost frightening how Bernard's words here describe some of the manifestations of sin in our world today, such as the insatiable desire for gratification and the tendency to give in to impulse rather than to act rationally and with moral restraint. It is no accident that such behavior is connected to an inability to distinguish between good and evil. Bernard is describing a person whose "conscience is dulled," which means that he or she has no fear of God. Ironically, this is one thing that the sinner has in common with the person who has attained pure humility:

Only at the top and at the bottom is there a free and effortless course, upward to life or downward to death; bounding on in the effortless energy of love, or hurried, unresisting, by the downward pull of cupidity. In one case love, in the other apathy ignores the labor of life. Perfect love or complete malice casts out fear. Security is found in truth or in blindness. (GH 21.51)

Remember that Bernard's context is the person who has "fallen" into this lowest state of pride. However, the goal of Christians is the opposite, to rise to the pinnacle of true humility before God. The moment one begins to have fear of the Lord, the habit of sin begins to be broken and humility becomes possible.

Benedict's second step of humility is not to love one's own will or to take pleasure in the satisfaction of one's desires (RB 7.31). Bernard contrasts this with freedom in sinning. In his view, this is what happens when a monk leaves or is expelled from the monastery:

The monk has no longer a superior to fear nor brethren to respect; so with fewer qualms he happily gives himself up to his sinful desires, which in the monastery fear and shame held in check. He has no abbot or fellow-religious to fear now, but he still keeps some scant fear of God. His conscience still gives some murmurs, however faint; he makes a few half-hearted resolutions, still hesitates a little in his first steps in evil. (GH 20.50)

For Benedict, it is not enough to know what God's will is or even to avoid acting contrary to it; humility grows when we begin to embrace God's will as more important than our own and actively seek it rather than our own satisfaction. Studying Bernard's words, we recognize the things that can begin to push pride out of our lives: a scant fear of God, a faint murmuring of conscience, and a few half-hearted resolutions.

How often do we find ourselves at such a stage? We are persons of faith and truly want to do God's will, yet the allure of sin and self-indulgence can often exert a powerful influence on us, and we fear that our faith is too weak to overcome it! As Paul says in Romans 7:19, "For I do not do the good I want, but the evil I do not want is what I do." But Paul also says, in 2 Corinthians 12:10, "whenever I am weak, then I am strong," because this moves us to rely on grace. Bernard understands that even a weak or half-hearted faith is enough of an opening for God's grace to work effectively in our lives.

For Bernard, the next logical step is to join a monastery of men or women. Indeed, Bernard is not afraid to plead vigorously for this. In his sermon to clerics *On Conversion,* he exclaims:

Spare your souls, brothers, I beg you, spare, spare the blood which has been poured out for you. Beware of the terrifying danger, turn away from the fire which has been made ready. . . . Can chastity remain unscathed amid delights, or humility among riches, or piety in business, or truth amid much talking, or charity in this present evil age? Flee from the midst of Babylon. Flee and save your souls! Flock to the city of refuge, where you can do penance for the past, obtain grace in the present, and confidently wait for future glory. (CO 21.37)

The "city of refuge" to which Bernard refers is none other than the monastery. With all due respect to those who have embraced the monastic life, today we might dispute that entering the monastery is necessarily the best way to progress further in the spiritual journey.

In fairness to Bernard, he does recognize that people who are not monks can experience the fullness of salvation. In one of his homilies in praise of the Virgin Mary, Bernard reflects on the description in Luke 1:26–27 of the angel Gabriel's visit to Mary. He notes how humility and virginity are united in Mary, then exhorts his readers:

If you are not able to imitate the virginity of this humble maid, then imitate the humility of the virgin maid. Virginity is a praiseworthy virtue, but humility is by far the more necessary. The one is only counselled; the other is demanded. To the first you have been invited; to the second you are obliged. . . . You can be saved without virginity; without humility you cannot be. (HL 1.5)

Humility in Relation to Human Authority

The next four steps of humility focus on the monk's relation to superiors. Benedict lists the third step of humility as submitting to one's superior in obedience for the love of God (RB 7:34). Bernard's corresponding step of pride is "rebellion against superiors and brethren."

All of us, whether we live in a monastery or not, will have to deal at some point with a human "superior," such as a supervisor, a teacher, or a parent. In the third step of humility, we move from submitting to God's will to submitting to the will of a human being who has authority over us. This was undoubtedly no easier in Bernard's time than it is in our own.

In this treatise, Bernard does not dwell at length on the possibility that a superior may make a wrong decision or deal harshly or unfairly with a member of the community, although he is certainly aware that this can be the case. As we saw in chapter 1, he recognized that he had treated one of his own siblings unfairly when he dismissed him from the monastery. In this treatise, Bernard generally assumes that the authority of superiors is exercised legitimately and that a monk should therefore submit to it.

At this stage of pride, a person may not have contempt for God, but "his contempt for superiors flashes out in open revolt" (GH 19.48). It is only with the help of God that we can overcome this tendency to reject all human authority. As Bernard puts it, "The divine mercy may yet rescue such a man and inspire him to submit to the judgment of the community" (GH 19.48). At the same time, Bernard recognizes that this submission involves our *consent*, as the dynamic of grace and freedom always does. It is all too easy to "take an attitude of brazen insolence" (GH 19.48).

Bernard asks, "If a monk refuses to live in harmony with his brethren or to obey his superior, what is he doing in the monastery except causing scandal?" (GH 19.49).

In applying Bernard's words to a context beyond that of the monastery, we might rephrase this last sentence as follows: "If people refuse to live in harmony with their brothers and sisters and to obey those who exercise authority, what are they doing in the community except causing scandal?" To live rightly in any community, monastic or otherwise, we have to let go of the idea that our will is always supreme. We need to be attentive to the needs and insights of others, including those in authority, and be willing at times to sacrifice our personal preferences for the sake of the common good. Otherwise, we end up tearing the community down rather than building it up.

Benedict's fourth step of humility is "that in this obedience under difficult, unfavorable, or even unjust conditions, [the monk's] heart quietly embraces suffering and endures it without weakening or seeking escape" (RB 7.35–36). It is interesting how Bernard summarizes this step: "to hold fast to patience amidst hard and rough things for the sake of obedience" (GH, table of contents).

Notice that Bernard does not mention in this summary statement the "unjust conditions" referred to by Benedict. One might be tempted to think that Bernard is conveniently ignoring or bracketing the problem of the illegitimate exercise of authority, but in his expanded description of a person at this stage of humility, he says:

A real penitent is not afraid of the difficulties of penance. Whatever is enjoined upon him for the fault which he hates, he patiently embraces with a quiet mind. If obedience should expose him to hard and mortifying things and *even undeserved reproaches* he will bear it unflinchingly. He has possession of the fourth degree of humility. (GH 17.47, emphasis added)

Bernard's mention of "undeserved reproaches" shows that he does recognize the "unjust conditions" to which Benedict refers. Nevertheless, at this stage of humility, monks are supposed to face their personal faults and accept whatever penance or mortification that their superiors deem necessary for them to grow in holiness.

The step of pride that contrasts with this patience is "hypocritical confession, which can be tested by harsh reproof." Bernard explains:

There are some who, when they are caught out in wrongdoing and know that if they defend themselves they will not be believed, find a subtle way out of the difficulty in deceitful self-accusation. This is the kind of man "who humbles himself deceitfully while his mind is full of evil" [Sirach 19:23]. . . . They will not merely admit what has happened but will exaggerate their guilt. They accuse themselves of things so great, so incredible, that you begin to doubt the charges you were certain of before. (GH 18.46)

This scenario presented by Bernard is not as far-fetched as it sounds. It is indeed possible sometimes to deflect criticism of sinful behavior by an excessive show of remorse. This often prompts the response, "Don't be so hard on yourself; what you did wasn't that bad."

But as soon as someone sees through the façade of humility and confronts the hypocrisy, the true colors of a person in this ninth stage of pride will be exposed:

The man whose penitence is fraudulent will show soon enough that it was a sham humility if he is given the slightest reproach or penance. He murmurs and growls and gets vexed. No, he is not in the fourth degree of humility but the ninth of pride which we have called hyp-ocritical confession. (GH 19.48)

Clearly, the path of humility is a rough one to follow, as our prideful instincts always threaten to pull us backward. At this stage, pride manifests itself as an attempt to escape from accountability, to get "off the hook." Few people relish the thought of having to make amends publicly for wrongdoings that they have committed. But growth in humility means learning to take responsibility for our actions.

Benedict's fifth step of humility is "that a man does not conceal from his abbot any sinful thoughts entering his heart, or any wrongs committed in secret, but rather confesses them humbly" (RB 7.44). Even harder than accepting a penance is admitting one's faults to begin with. Thus, the corresponding eighth step of pride is "defending one's sins." Bernard reviews some of the common ways in which people excuse their sins, none of which, we should note, are confined to monasteries:

One will say: "I didn't do it." Another: "I did it, but I was perfectly right in doing it." If it was wrong he may say: "It isn't all that bad." If it was decidedly harmful, he can fall back on: "I meant well." If the bad intention is too evident he will take refuge in the excuses of Adam and Eve and say someone else led him into it. (GH 17.45)

Several centuries later, these and other excuses are alive and well. It is not easy to say, "I was wrong." But the person who is growing in humility is able to take this step.

One complicating factor in our own day, which was not a major issue in Bernard's time, is that there are some who would minimize or deny any distinction between right and wrong. So instead of saying that an evil action "isn't all that bad," they say, "It isn't bad at all; in fact, nothing you can do is really bad." This is not the place to enter into a discussion of the relativism that afflicts our postmodern world, but we might consider whether this denial of all moral standards only illustrates Bernard's point, rather than nullifies it.

Benedict's sixth step of humility is "that a monk is content with the lowest and most menial treatment, and regards himself as a poor and worthless workman in whatever task he is given" (RB 7.49). Bernard's contrasting step of pride is "meddling with everything," or acting on the presumption that one is better than others. Bernard asks:

When a man thinks he is better than others will he not put himself before others? He must have the first place in gatherings, be the first to speak in council. He comes without being called. He interferes without being asked. He must rearrange everything, re-do whatever has been done. What he himself did not do or arrange is not rightly done or properly arranged. He is the judge of all judges and decides every case beforehand. If he is not made Prior when a vacancy occurs he knows that the Abbot is jealous of him, or has been deceived! If obedience calls him to some ordinary task, he refuses disdainfully. (GH 16.44)

From the very beginning, Christianity has taught that those who wish to attain greatness should take the lowest place. Jesus himself proclaimed this continually by both word and example. Recall his words in the gospels: "Whoever wishes to become great among you must be your servant, and whoever wishes to be first among you must be slave of all" (Mark 10:43-44). "When you are invited, go and sit down at the lowest place, so that when your host comes, he may say to you, 'Friend, move up higher'; then you will be honored in the presence of all who sit at the table with you. For all who exalt themselves will be humbled, and those who humble themselves will be exalted" (Luke 14:10-11).

Thus, the next step of humility takes us beyond confession of our sins to confession of our unworthiness; in particular, to letting go of our desire to be in a position of power or control. This means being willing to take the lowest place and not regarding any task as "below our dignity." Remember that Bernard is still focused here on the relationship to superiors. Who of us has not at one time or another been seduced by the desire for power, or thought that we were more deserving of a position of authority than the one who holds it? Such a desire is rooted in the prior conviction of our superiority to others. Addressing this misguided conviction brings us into the final arena of growth in humility, learning to be humble in relation to our brothers and sisters in community.

Humility in Relation to the Community

St. Benedict states, "The seventh step of humility is that a man not only admits with his tongue but is also convinced in his heart that he is inferior to all and of less value" (RB 7.51). Bernard contrasts this with "self-assertion; believing one is holier than others":

He swallows all the praise others give him. He is quite complacent about his conduct and he never examines his motives now; the good opinion of others is all he needs. About everything else he thinks he knows more than anybody, but when they say something favorable about him he believes them against his own conscience. So now not only in words and affected conduct does he display his piety but he believes in his inmost heart that he is holier than others. (GH 15.43)

If the sixth level of humility entails letting go of the desire to be "in charge," this seventh level carries us one step further, where we face our own pretenses to being holier than we actually are. This does not mean that we should deny the genuine goodness that exists within us. But Bernard is convinced that our natural tendency is to look too highly upon ourselves.

Many feminist thinkers today would challenge Bernard on this point, saying that this tendency to have overblown egos may be characteristic of men, but it is not generally so of women. They claim that women have more often erred in not recognizing and embracing their innate dignity and their giftedness and, consequently, have allowed themselves to be oppressed and marginalized.

It may very well be that women have tended not to look upon themselves highly enough. Let us remember that Bernard believes humility must be based on the truth. The challenge for many women is to recognize the goodness and talent that they have too often ignored. Nevertheless, all human beings, men and women alike, are capable of the pride of self-assertion. At this level of humility, each person must enter into an honest internal dialogue to ask whether the shoe fits.

Once we have faced honestly our false pretenses of holiness (or of the lack of it), we can grow further by manifesting humility outwardly by the way we live in community. Bernard sees the honest self-assessment of the seventh step as only gradually coming to fruition in day-to-day living. Indeed, Bernard confronts the pride that can exist at these last stages with a harshness that may seem excessive, since presumably pride is less intense toward the top of the "staircase." The only explanation I can offer for this is that Bernard seems to think of pride as something that "snow-balls." Once we allow pride to enter our hearts, at whatever level, it becomes easier for it to take over and drag us inexorably downward.

Benedict's eighth step of humility is "that a monk does only what is endorsed by the common rule of the monastery and the example set by his superiors" (RB 7.55). Bernard contrasts this with "singularity, proud esteem of one's own ways."

The first step beyond recognizing our lowliness is being willing to submit to the guidelines of community living. But at this stage, pride can manifest itself in a desire to do "more"—or really something *other*—than what is required, in order to be seen as more humble:

The common rule of the monastery and the example of the seniors are no longer enough for [the monk at this stage of pride]. . . . He is not so much concerned about leading a better life as appearing to others to do so. . . . While he is at his meals he casts his eyes around the tables and if he sees anyone eating less than himself he is mortified at being outdone and promptly and cruelly deprives himself even of necessary food. He would rather starve his body than his pride. (GH 14.42)

One of the litmus tests of higher humility is thus to ask ourselves how much we are still concerned with appearances, with showing others how humble we are. Bernard thinks that a person at this stage of pride becomes "very exact about his own particular doings and slack about the common exercises" (GH 14.42). In other words, one begins to pursue holiness in isolation from the rest of the community rather than in solidarity with others. This is not to say that having a personal spirituality is wrong. But spirituality grows in the context of community living. In Bernard's time, as now, "privatized spirituality" is a contradiction in terms.

Benedict's ninth step of humility is "that a monk controls his tongue and remains silent, not speaking unless asked a question" (RB 7.56). Bernard contrasts this with "boasting and too much talking." A monk caught in this stage of pride

is not shy about producing his opinions; words are bubbling over. He does not wait to be asked. His information comes before any question. He asks the questions; gives the answers; cuts off anyone who tries to speak. . . . He may have the capacity to help others but that is the least of his concerns. His aim is not to teach you nor to be taught by you, but to show how much he knows. . . . To say it briefly, when words are many, boasting is not lacking. (GH 13.41)

So, to progress even further in humility, it is not only necessary to stop making a show of "humble" observances, it is also necessary to stop showing off our knowledge. In a highly educated society such as our own, these words of Bernard have perhaps an even greater sting than they did in the monastery.

Benedict's tenth step of humility is "that [the monk] is not given to ready laughter" (RB 7.59). Bernard's corresponding step of pride is "silly mirth, with over-much laughing." Notice the qualifiers here. Bernard does not seem to be against humor per se, but only "ready" laughter, "over-much" laughing. What is at the root of his concern here?

Watch such a man and you will never notice anything like a tear or a sigh. His appearance is that of a man who is forgetful of what he is or at least is now purified of all trace of sin. He is scurrilous in sign-making, over-cheerful in appearance, swaggering in his bearing, always ready for a joke; any little thing quickly gets a laugh (GH 12.40).

In his treatise *Grace and Free Choice*, Bernard refers to such giddiness as "false joy," which comes from hoping in ourselves rather than in God (DG 5.14). In other words, his concern is that humor can become a means of refusing to face our sins or our shortcomings. The person who is growing in humility, on the other hand, has a joy that is rooted in God.

It may be more clear to consider the last two stages of humility together. Benedict's eleventh step of humility is "that a monk speaks gently and without laughter, seriously and with becoming modesty, briefly and reasonably, but without raising his voice" (RB 7.60). His final step is "that a monk always manifests humility in his bearing no less than in his heart" (RB 7.62).

For Benedict and Bernard, people attain the fullness of humility when it is manifested both internally and externally, in their hearts and in their external behaviors. The truly humble person is totally focused on God. Benedict describes the state of such a person as follows:

> After ascending all these steps of humility, the monk will quickly arrive at that perfect love of God which casts out fear [1 John 4:18]. Through this love, all that he once performed with dread, he will now begin to observe without effort, as though naturally, from habit, no longer out of fear of hell, but out of love for Christ, good habit, and delight in virtue. All this the Lord will by the Holy Spirit graciously manifest in his workman now cleansed of vices and sins. (RB 7.67-70)

As we have seen, Bernard expands on this insight by speaking of the three degrees of truth, which embrace love, humility itself, and contemplation. Whether we can fully enjoy these gifts in our present life is a question we will return to in the next chapter.

What is the foundational catalyst for falling from humility into pride? Bernard calls it "curiosity: when the eyes and the other senses attend to what is not one's concern." He explains:

You see one who up to this time had every appearance of being an excellent monk. Now you begin to notice that wherever he is, standing, walking, or sitting, his eyes are wandering, his glance darts right and left, his ears are cocked. Some change has taken place in him; every movement shows it. . . . He used to watch over his own conduct; now all his watchfulness is for others. (GH 10.28)

We might at this point ask: Aren't we talking about a person who has reached the summit of humility? How is it possible that such a person would fall? Maybe this is the key to understanding why Bernard develops his treatise as he does, explaining the way down rather than the way up. Bernard knows that even a person who has made great progress in the spiritual life, who has attained a high level of personal holiness, is capable of slipping backward. And what does it take to start careening down this slippery slope? Not much—only the urge to compare ourselves with others and to start meddling in things that don't concern us.

Indeed, Bernard suggests that it was really curiosity that was behind the original sin in the Garden of Eden. He theorizes what Eve was thinking about when she regarded the forbidden fruit:

You are forbidden to eat that fruit, why do you look at it? "Oh!" you answer, "I am only looking. I have not so much as put a hand to it. My eyes are under no restriction; I was forbidden only to eat. What did God give me eyes for if I cannot look at whatever I want?" (GH 10.30)

Bernard sees this look as the occasion of sin:

The look may not have been a sin itself but there was a sin somewhere in the background. You cannot have been watching very carefully over yourself or you would not have had time for this curiosity. It may not itself be a sin but it is leading you on to sin. You are already guilty of some fault in the matter and more will follow. (GH 10.30)

Bernard thinks that once the eyes start wandering, the mind will soon follow. Thus he describes the second step of pride as "levity of mind, known by words that bespeak unreasonable joy and sadness":

The monk who observes others instead of attending to himself will begin before long to see some as his superiors and others as his inferiors; in some he will see things to envy, in others, things to despise. . . . [The mind] is no longer steadily fixed on its real concerns and is now carried up on the crest of the waves of pride, now down in the trough of envy. One minute the man is full of envious sadness, the next childishly glad about some excellence he sees in himself. The former is evil, the latter, vain; both bespeak pride because it is love of one's own excellence that makes one weep when he is surpassed and rejoice in surpassing others. (GH 11.39)

In other words, once curiosity sets in, it is easy to slip into envy and narcissism, and then to slip further into "silly mirth," and so on down the line. Once one steps onto the ladder of pride, it becomes progressively easier to descend the later steps.

At each stage, however, there is also the possibility of shifting back to a stance of humility. This is what I have tried to extrapolate from Bernard's exposition of the steps of pride.

The Significance of Bernard's Treatise

Let us summarize the insights on growth in humility that we have culled from Bernard's treatise:

1. Cultivate a constant awareness of God's presence and God's commandments.

2. Actively seek God's will rather than your own.

3. Be attentive to the needs and insights of others, including those in authority, and be willing to sacrifice your personal preferences for the sake of the common good.

4. Be accountable: take responsibility for your mistakes, and be willing to make amends for them.

5. Have the courage to admit your faults. Learn how to say "I was wrong."

6. Let go of the desire for power or control. Be willing to take the lowest place and to perform mundane tasks.

7. Don't think of yourself as better or holier than you are. Don't think of yourself as worse either. Face the truth about yourself.

8. Don't pit your personal spirituality against that of the community. Be willing to recognize the community's wisdom and follow its guidelines for living.

9. Do not show off your knowledge to others.

10. Make sure your joy is anchored in God. Don't use humor as a means of avoiding facing the truth about yourself.

11. Be modest in all your speech and behavior.

12. Focus your attention on God; make God the center of your life, both internally and in your external behavior.

It should be clear at this point why Bernard sees conversion as a lifelong process. The things we must do to make progress in humility are truly a tall order. Bernard thinks we must constantly be vigilant about our spiritual life. There is no such thing as being in a holding pattern. In this connection, he once said to a group of abbots: "Either you must go up or you must come down; you inevitably fall if you try to stand still" (LB 94.2).

Obviously, there are many issues related to conversion that Benedict and Bernard have not covered in these texts. For example, they do not develop at length here the component of service to others. It is certainly implied that growth in humility entails the willingness to serve (e.g., being willing to perform menial tasks for the good of the community), but we are left hungering for more detail about how service relates to conversion. This dimension comes out more strongly in Bernard's treatise on the love of God, the next text in our survey.

As noted above, Bernard sees our growth in conversion as leading us to three levels of truth. In this chapter, we have focused on the first of these, humility. The next two chapters will focus on the other two levels: love and contemplation.

Chapter 4

The Love of God

We have already noted that Bernard has much to say about freedom. He has even more to say about another central aspect of human existence: love. Like freedom, love is a word that admits of many different levels and meanings. Bernard is interested in talking about love in its highest sense, which is loving God so totally that we do not even think of ourselves. But he recognizes that this kind of love is the fruit of a lifelong journey, during which we grow through several important stages. Indeed, Bernard believes that the fullness of love, with very few exceptions, will be experienced only in the afterlife.

The theme of love permeates many of Bernard's writings, but none so fully as his treatise *On Loving God* (*De diligendo Deo*) and his *Sermons on the Song of Songs* (*Sermones super Cantica canticorum*). In this chapter, we will focus on the first of these works. In the next chapter, we will turn to the *Sermons on the Song of Songs* and focus on the relationship between love and mystical union.

Bernard probably wrote his treatise *On Loving God* sometime after 1125. He addressed it to Cardinal Haimeric, who was one of Bernard's friends and supporters in Rome. We mentioned him in chapter 1 in relation to the disputed election of Pope Innocent II.

Why God Should Be Loved

As in his treatise on grace and free choice, Bernard begins his treatise on love with a succinct statement of his thesis, which he then proceeds to expand:

You wish me to tell you why and how God should be loved. My answer is that God himself is the reason why he should be loved. As for how he is to be loved, there is to be no limit to that love. Is this sufficient answer? . . . [F]or the sake of those who are slow to grasp ideas I do not find it burdensome to treat of the same ideas more extensively if not more profoundly. Hence I insist that there are two reasons why God should be loved for his own sake: no one can be loved more righteously and no one can be loved with greater benefit. (DD 1.1)

Bernard's main focus in this treatise is on our love for God rather than on God's love for us. He has a good deal to say, however, about the latter as well. God deserves our love because of the boundless love that he has shown for us.

God certainly deserves a lot from us since he gave himself to us when we deserved it least. Besides, what could he give us better than himself? Hence when seeking why God should be loved, if one asks what right he has to be loved, the answer is that the main reason for loving him is "He loved us first" [1 John 4:9-10]. Surely he is worthy of being loved in return when one thinks of who loves, whom he loves, how much he loves. . . . This divine love is sincere, for it is the love of one who does not seek his own advantage. (DD 1.1)

Notice here the emphasis on the *selfless* quality of God's love. The highest form of love, for Bernard, is love that does not seek its own advantage. The entire treatise revolves around this conception.

Bernard goes on to specify the "innumerable gifts" that God places at our disposal:

For, who else gives food to all who eat, sight to all who see, and air to all who breathe? It would be foolish to want to enumerate; what I have just said cannot be counted. It suffices to point out the chief ones: bread, sun, and air. I call them the chief gifts, not because they are better but because the body cannot live without them. Man's nobler gifts—dignity, knowledge, and virtue—are found in the higher part of his being, in his soul. Man's dignity is his free will by which he is superior to the beasts and even dominates them. His knowledge is that by which he acknowledges that this dignity is in him but that it is not of his own making. Virtue is that by which man seeks continuously and eagerly for his Maker and when he finds him, adheres to him with all his might. (DD 2.2)

Let us pause here and consider the richness of what Bernard has just said. Bread, sun, and air: how often do we forget to thank God for these fundamental gifts that bring us life? But Bernard does not stop here. He talks about the nobler gifts that God has bestowed on human beings: dignity, knowledge, and virtue. Notice that Bernard connects human dignity with free will, which we discussed in chapter two. We know that this dignity is itself a gift from God. Virtue, whereby we seek and cling to God, is also a gift. In other words, Bernard proclaims here the same point that he makes in *De gratia*, that all of what we experience in life is finally grace. To put it plainly, God gives us everything we have, both materially and spiritually. Such boundless generosity surely deserves a loving response.

Bernard is not content to make this point once. He wants to be sure that people give proper credit to God for their dignity, knowledge, and virtue:

[D]ignity without knowledge is unprofitable, without virtue it can be an obstacle. The following reasoning explains both these facts. What glory is there in having something you do not know you have? Then, to know what you have but to be ignorant of the fact that you do not have it of yourself, for glory here, but not before God. The Apostle says to him who glorifies himself, "What have you that you have not received? And if you have received it, how can you boast of it as if you had not received it?" [1 Corinthians 4:7] (DD 2.3)

It should be noted that Bernard is not trying to denigrate the human race here. On the contrary, he sees human beings as God's greatest creation, but he also knows how easy it is to forget the source of our greatness:

There are two facts you should know: first, what you are; secondly, that you are not that by your own power, lest you fail to boast at all or do so in vain. . . . We should . . . fear that ignorance which gives us a too low opinion of ourselves. But we should fear no less, but rather more, that which makes us think ourselves better than we are. This is what happens when we deceive ourselves thinking some good is in us of ourselves. . . . It is pride, the greatest of sins, to use gifts as if they were one's by natural right and while receiving benefits to usurp the benefactor's glory. (DD 2.4)

This kind of language is no doubt offensive to our late-twentieth-century ears. We like to think of ourselves as self-made people who deserve all the credit for our accomplishments, and we generally consider a low self-image as much more to be feared than a high one. The result is that pride and arrogance run rampant in our society. Ironically, they often exist side by side with an inner insecurity about our self-worth.

Perhaps Bernard is more correct in his approach than we would care to admit. In this whole treatise, and elsewhere, he encourages us to "let go" of possessiveness. He is not referring in this instance to material things but rather to a self-possessive or narcissistic attitude. When Bernard says we should know "what we are," he means we should accept the goodness in ourselves, even as we glorify the God of love for making us good. According to Bernard, this is not a denial of our own self-worth but rather a more honest and truthful way of affirming it.

The Way of the Wicked vs. the Way of the Just

It is inconceivable to Bernard that anyone would be unaware of the divine gifts he has described or would not sense the need to love God in gratitude for them:

Is there an infidel who does not know that he has received the necessities for bodily life, by which he exists, sees, and breathes, from him who gives food to all flesh, who makes his sun rise on the good and the bad, and his rain fall on the just and the unjust? Who, again, can be wicked enough to think the author of his human dignity, which shines in his soul, is any other than he who says in the book of Genesis: "Let us make man to our own image and likeness"? Who can think that the giver of knowledge is somebody different from him who teaches man knowledge? Or again, who believes he has received or hopes to receive the gift of virtue from any other source than the hand of the Lord of virtue? Hence God deserves to be loved for his own sake even by the infidel who, although he is ignorant of Christ yet knows himself. Everyone, therefore, even the infidel, is inexcusable if he fails to love the Lord his God with all his heart, all his soul, all his might. For an innate justice, not unknown to reason, cries interiorly to him that he ought to love with his whole being the one to whom he owes all that he is. (DD 2.6)

In our own day, of course, there *are* those who would deny that any of these gifts come from God, even the material ones. This was rarely, if ever, the case in Bernard's time. Bernard and his medieval contemporaries took the teaching of Romans 1:20 at its word: "Ever since the creation of the world [God's] eternal power and divine nature, invisible though they are, have been understood and seen through the things he has made." But even in Bernard's time, people did not necessarily follow through on the implications of this perception. Thus, Bernard goes on to talk at some length about two kinds of people: the wicked and the faithful. Although this is a bit of a digression from Bernard's main point in the treatise, it is one worth reviewing because of its relevance to our spiritual lives today.

Who are the wicked for Bernard? The answer will not be a welcome one in our affluent, consumption-driven society. They are generally defined as those whose main goal in life is to make money. Bernard laments their wanting to have it both ways: "O wretched slaves of Mammon, you cannot glory in the Cross of our Lord Jesus Christ and at the same time trust in hoards of money or chase after gold and taste how sweet is the Lord" (DD 4.12). He later argues that seeking the pleasures of this life is an exercise in futility, because we will never be satisfied:

A man with a beautiful wife, for example, looks at a more attractive woman with a wanton eye or heart; a well dressed man wants more costly clothes; and a man of great wealth envies anyone richer than he. You can see men who already own many farms and possessions, still busy, day after day, adding one field to another, driven by an excessive passion to extend their holdings. You can see men living in homes worthy of a king and in sumptuous dwellings, none the less daily adding house to house, through restless curiosity building up, then tearing down, changing squares into circles. What about men promoted to high honors? Do we not see them striving more and more in an insatiable ambition to go higher still? There is no end to all this, because no single one of these riches can be held to be the highest or the best. . . . Thus the restless mind, running to and fro among the pleasures of this life, is tired out but never satisfied; like the starving man who thinks whatever he stuffs down his throat is not enough, for his eyes see what remains to be eaten. . . . Who can have everything? (DD 7.18)

This description of insatiable desires could have as easily been written yesterday as in the twelfth century. Bernard asks, "Who can have everything?" But in his day as in ours, there were people who wanted to have it all, in the material sense, and yet who remained unfulfilled. In Bernard's view, these people were backing the wrong horse:

The wicked, therefore, walk round in circles, naturally wanting whatever will satisfy their desires, yet foolishly rejecting that which would lead them to their true end, which is not in consumption but in consummation. Hence they exhaust themselves in vain instead of perfecting their lives by a blessed end. They take more pleasure in the appearance of things than in their Creator, examining all and wanting to test them one by one before trying to reach the Lord of the universe. They might even succeed in doing so if they could ever gain hold of what they wish for; that is, if any one man could take possession of all things without him who is their Principle. By the very law of man's desire which makes him want what he lacks in place of what he has and grow weary of what he has in preference to what he lacks, once he has obtained and despised all in heaven on earth, he will hasten toward the only one who is missing, the God of all. . . . This is altogether impossible because life is too short, strength too weak, competition too keen, men too fatigued by the long road and vain efforts; wishing to attain all they desire, yet unable to reach the end of all their wants. (DD 7.19-20)

Notice here Bernard's belief that even *if* people who seek after the things of this world could ever "have it all," they would come to despise it and finally turn to God. But Bernard thinks life is too short and the wicked too obsessed with their worldly goals for this ever to happen. Thus, the wicked are doomed to frustration. Bernard asks, "When will they reach him whom they do not want to reach until they have tested all the rest? . . . The desire to experience all things first is like a vicious circle, it goes on forever." (DD 7.20)

In sharp contrast, Bernard speaks of the just, those whose main goal in life is to be faithful to God in love. If even infidels are aware that they owe everything to God, how much more, Bernard says, will the faithful recognize how deserving God is of our love. Bernard speaks of the two graces that God gives us in this life: creation and redemption, a theme we saw earlier in his work on grace and free choice:

If I owe all I have for being created, what can I add for being remade, and being remade in this way? It was less easy to remake me than to make me. It is written not only about me but of every created being, "He spoke and they were made" [Psalm 148:2]. But he who made me by a single word, in remaking me had to speak many words, work miracles, suffer hardships, and not only hardships but even unjust treatment. "What shall I render to the Lord for all that he has given me?" [Psalm 115:2]. In the first work he gave me myself; in his second work he gave me himself; when he gave me himself, he gave me back myself. Given and regiven, I owe myself twice over. What can I give God in return for himself? Even if I could give him myself a thousand times, what am I to God? (DD 5.15)

Bernard is still giving his answer to the first question, why God should be loved. God deserves our love because his love for us has been so generous, even more so in redeeming us than in creating us. Bernard marvels over the contrast between the single word that brought us into being (see Genesis 1:26) and the many words and deeds of Jesus that were necessary for our redemption. He sums up the significance of this in a powerful phrase, "I owe myself twice over."

I noted above that this section on the wicked and the just is a digression. It is not unusual for Bernard to take a long time to get to the heart of his argument. In fact, he is well aware of his tendency to get off track, and he will often state, after a lengthy digression or an overlong discussion of an ancillary point, that he needs to get back to the subject.

How God Should Be Loved

Bernard finally moves to his second point, how God should be loved. In the light of God's overwhelming love for us, Bernard calls us to try to love God back in the same manner. What begins as an exhortation to his readers suddenly shifts into a prayer:

Such a one loved us so much and so freely, insignificant as we are and such as we are, that, as you recall I said

in the beginning, we must love God without any limit. . . .
My God, my help, I shall love you as much as I am able
for your gift. My love is less than your due, yet not less
than I am able, for even if I cannot love you as much as
I should, still I cannot love you more than I can. I shall
only be able to love you more when you give me more,
although you can never find my love worthy of you. (DD
6.16)

Bernard here reprises the theme we saw in the last chapter:
our Christian life is an ongoing process of conversion. We
never reach the point in this life where we can say, "I love
God enough."

Before he proceeds to expound the stages of loving God,
Bernard makes one last preliminary point: that our love for
God will be amply rewarded. This may seem unusual in a
treatise whose emphasis is on selfless love, but this for
Bernard is the great paradox. The person who loves God
unselfishly will reap rich rewards. Bernard is careful to
insist that "true love merits its reward, it does not seek it."
Although it is true that God is not loved without reward,
"he should be loved without regard for one." Bernard asks:

Who would dream of offering a man a reward for doing
something he wants to do? No one, for example, pays a
hungry man to eat, a thirsty man to drink, or a mother
to feed the child of her womb. Who would think of using
prayers or prizes to remind a man to fence in his vine,
to dig around his tree, or to build his own home? How
much more the soul that loves God seeks no other
reward than that God whom it loves. Were the soul to
demand anything else, then it would certainly love that
other thing and not God. (DD 7.17)

Here Bernard is being true to his Benedictine roots, in
which the desire for God is ultimately the only desire that

will be satisfied, though not fully in this life, as we shall see.

Bernard now moves to the heart of his treatise, a discussion of the four degrees of love through which we progress in our spiritual life. In the first degree, human beings love themselves for their own sake. In the second, they love God for their own sake. In the third, they love God for God's sake, and in the fourth, they love even themselves for God's sake. This schema may seem a bit artificial, and I suspect that Bernard himself did not think of love as always developing in so neat and tidy a fashion. Nevertheless, Bernard's descriptions show genuine insight into the process that takes place when love becomes more mature.

Bernard describes the first degree of love, loving ourselves for our own sake, as follows:

Since nature has become more fragile and weak, necessity obliges man to serve it first. This is carnal love by which a man loves himself above all for his own sake. He is only aware of himself; as St. Paul says: "What was animal came first, then what was spiritual" [1 Corinthians 15:46]. Love is not imposed by a precept; it is placed in nature. Who is there who hates his own flesh? Yet should love, as it happens, grow immoderate, and, like a savage current, burst the banks of necessity, flooding the fields of delight, the overflow is immediately stopped by the commandment which says: "You shall love your neighbor as yourself" [Matthew 22:39]. . . . Should a man feel overburdened at satisfying not only his brethren's just needs but also their pleasures, let him restrain his own if he does not want to be a transgressor. He can be indulgent as he likes for himself providing he remembers his neighbor has the same rights. . . . Then your love will be sober and just if you do not refuse your brother that which he needs of what you have denied yourself in pleasure. Thus carnal love becomes social when it is extended to others. (DD 8.23)

The first thing we should note in relation to this passage is that Bernard does not give us a schema that moves from bad to good. The first stage of love, in which we love our own bodily selves, is necessary because our human nature has become "weak and fragile" through sin. There is nothing bad about this love per se. There is a danger, of course, that it will blossom into self-indulgence, but remember that Bernard's context here is a description of people who are on the road to faithfulness and justice.

Such people, selfish though their love may be at this stage, at least recognize that their neighbors have the same "just needs" as themselves. So, ideally, they are moved to deny themselves certain "pleasures" (wants) in order to give their neighbors what they need. Bernard does not speak here of maintaining a pleasurable lifestyle and giving to others out of our surplus but rather of *denying* ourselves what is superfluous in order that others might have what is necessary.

Thus, even carnal love, when it becomes social, can be quite a challenge. As we saw earlier in the treatise, Bernard is well aware of how self-indulgence can become a vicious cycle where people just want more and more for themselves. And he was not living in the industrialized, consumerist society that we are! Bernard is convinced that, finally, we will not be able to meet this challenge until we bring God into the picture:

[I]n order to love one's neighbor with perfect justice, one must have regard to God. In other words, how can one love one's neighbor with purity, if one does not love him in God? But it is impossible to love in God unless one loves God. It is necessary, therefore, to love God first;

then one can love one's neighbor in God. . . . In this way, man who is animal and carnal, and knows how to love only himself, yet starts loving God for his own benefit, because he learns from frequent experience that he can do everything that is good for him in God and that without God he can do nothing good. (DD 8.25)

And so, Bernard moves to the second degree of love, where we love God for our own benefit. Bernard devotes just a short paragraph to this stage:

Man, therefore, loves God, but for his own advantage and not yet for God's sake. Nevertheless, it is a matter of prudence to know what you can do by yourself and what you can do with God's help to keep from offending him who keeps you free from sin. If man's tribulations, however, grow in frequency and as a result he frequently turns to God and is frequently freed by God, must he not end, even though he had a heart of stone in a breast of iron, by realizing that it is God's grace which frees him and come to love God not for his own advantage but for the sake of God? (DD 9.26)

In essence, Bernard is arguing here that God's mercy and generosity will sooner or later melt even the hardest of hearts. Inspired by God's selfless love, we will finally begin to move beyond our own self-centeredness and begin to love God for God's sake. As Bernard eloquently puts it, "tasting God's sweetness entices us more to pure love than does the urgency of our own needs" (DD 9.26).

This third degree of love, although its focus is on loving God for God's sake, also brings us to the point where we can fully love our neighbor. For now we can love as God loves: unselfishly.

[A person in the third stage of love] loves God truthfully and so loves what is God's. He loves purely and he does not find it hard to obey a pure commandment, purifying his heart, as it is written, in the obedience of love. He loves with justice and freely embraces the just commandment. This love is pleasing because it is free. It is chaste because it does not consist of spoken words but of deed and truth. It is just because it renders what is received. Whoever loves this way, loves the way he is loved, seeking in turn not what is his but what belongs to Christ, the same way Christ sought not what was his, but what was ours, or rather, ourselves. He so loves who says: "Confess to the Lord for he is good" [Psalm 117:1]. Who confesses to the Lord, not because he is good to him but because the Lord is good, truly loves God for God's sake and not for his own benefit. (DD 9.26)

Bernard believes that, in general, this third degree is the highest stage of love that people will experience in this life. He begins his discussion of the fourth degree of love by saying:

Happy the man who has attained the fourth degree of love, he no longer even loves himself except for God. . . . I would say that a man is blessed and holy to whom it is given to experience something of this sort, so rare in life, even if it be but once and for the space of a moment. To lose yourself, as if you no longer existed, to cease completely to experience yourself, to reduce yourself to nothing is not a human sentiment but a divine experience. (DD 10.27)

There are two things to take note of here: first, Bernard sees the fourth degree of love as a grace, something we are "given to experience." It is not something we can bring about by our own efforts (see DD 10.29). Second, Bernard suggests, at least in this passage, that it is *possible* to experience the fourth degree of love during our earthly life, though in a rare and fleeting way. He goes on to say that the martyrs may have experienced it "at least partially" while they were still in their bodies (DD 10.29). In one of his sermons on the Song of Songs, he outrightly admits that he has had such an experience himself. So Bernard seems to think that this degree of love can at least be tasted by martyrs and contemplatives.

On the other hand, in a letter that is appended to the end of the treatise on loving God, Bernard expresses doubt that *anyone* "ever attains the fourth degree during this life, that is, if he [or she] ever loves only for God's sake. Let those who have had the experience make a statement; for me, I confess, it seems impossible" (DD 15.40). It may be that Bernard wrote this letter before having his own experience of mystical love.

What is more fascinating is how Bernard describes the nature of this degree of love. Here we enter the realm of what is usually called "mystical union," a topic we will be discussing further in the next chapter. This degree of love brings us as close to God as it is possible for a human being:

It is therefore necessary for our souls to reach a similar state in which, just as God willed everything to exist for himself, so we wish that neither ourselves nor other beings to have been nor to be except for his will alone, not for our pleasure. The satisfaction of our wants, chance happiness, delights us less than to see his will done in us and for us, which we implore every day in prayer saying, ". . . your will be done on earth as it is in heaven" [Matthew 6:10]. . . . It is deifying to go through such an experience. As a drop of water seems to disappear completely in a big quantity of wine, even assuming the wine's taste and color; just as red, molten iron becomes so much like fire it seems to lose its primary state; just as the air on a sunny day seems transformed into sunshine instead of being lit up; so it is necessary

for the saints that all human feelings melt in a mysterious way and flow into the will of God. Otherwise, how
will God be all in all if something human survives in man?
No doubt, the substance remains though under another
form, another glory, another power. (DD 10.28)

Bernard conceives of mystical union as a union with God
in love. This is often called a "relational" concept of union
as opposed to an "essential" one in which union is
described in terms of an annihilation of the self or a total
absorption into God. It does seem, at first glance, that
Bernard understands the union more in the essential sense.
But look again at the passage above, and notice how carefully Bernard chooses his words. The drop of water *seems* to
disappear in the wine; the molten iron *seems* to lose its primary state, and the air *seems* to be transformed into sunshine. And human *feelings* (not our humanity itself) melt
and flow into the *will* of God, not God's own substance per
se. To make sure this is clear, Bernard adds that the *substance
of our humanity remains*, though it is under another form,
glory, and power.

Bernard repeats that the highest degree of love is generally not attained in this life. In fact, it is not immediately
obtained in the afterlife either. Bernard holds the traditional belief that at death, souls are separated from their
bodies, but they are reunited with their bodies at the time
of the final resurrection. He explains:

But if . . . [souls] wish that they had received their bodies back or certainly if they desire and hope to receive
them, there is no doubt that they have not altogether
turned from themselves, for it is clear they still cling to
something of their own to which their desires return
though ever so slightly. Consequently, until death is swal-
lowed up in victory and eternal light invades from all
sides the limits of night and takes possession to the

extent that heavenly glory shines in their bodies, souls cannot set themselves aside and pass into God. They are still attached to their bodies, if not by life and feeling, certainly by a natural affection, so that they do not wish nor are they able to realize their consummation without them. This rapture of the soul which is its most perfect and highest state, cannot, therefore, take place before the resurrection of the bodies, lest the spirit, if it could reach perfection without the body, would no longer desire to be united to the flesh. (DD 11.31)

Modern theologians tend not to speak of the body and soul in such a bifurcated way. In any case, Bernard's point is that we cannot enter fully into this highest experience of love until no distractions remain that keep us preoccupied with ourselves. When body and soul are reunited, "we shall be filled with everlasting life, abounding in a wonderful fullness." God will "intoxicate" us with love:

At last, here is that sober intoxication of truth, not from overdrinking, not reeking with wine, but burning for God. From this then that fourth degree of love is possessed forever, when God alone is loved in the highest way, for now we do not love ourselves except for his sake, that he may be the reward of those who love him, the eternal recompense of those who love him forever. (DD 11.33)

This final degree of love is enjoyed for all eternity. Notice how Bernard describes it as a "burning for God." This is the same flame of desire that exists for believers in an imperfect way in this life, especially, Bernard would say, in the life of a monk.

The Significance of Bernard's Treatise

Bernard reminds us today, as he reminded his readers in the twelfth century, that love in its highest manifestations is selfless. This is an important message for a society in which self-absorption is shamelessly promoted and encouraged. Even in discussing the lowest degree of love, which he sees as steeped in selfishness, Bernard raises challenges to a world in which the rich are getting richer and the poor are getting poorer. He asks us how we can justify catering to our every want when many of our neighbors are crying out in desperate need. He has the boldness to suggest that we should deny ourselves what is superfluous in order that others may have what is necessary. His point here is similar to a contemporary slogan used by many advocates of social justice when they call people "to live simply that others may simply live." Bernard does not see this as a heroic accomplishment but as an expression of basic human decency, granting others the same fundamental human rights that we claim for ourselves.

The move from self-centered to self-giving love is a difficult one to make. We often learn the hard way, through destructive relationships that are centered more on our own need for fulfillment and satisfaction than on genuine caring and reverence for the other. Bernard presents God's love as the paradigm that we should be emulating, learning how to love as God loved us. Imagine what would happen if all of our manifestations of human love, including the romantic ones, were rooted in Bernard's model of divine love, and not in the shallow and sentimental model of love that is advanced by today's entertainment industry.

The miracle is that when we stop worrying about our own fulfillment in love, that is precisely when we find the fulfillment that has been eluding us. As a well-known prayer that is incorrectly attributed to St. Francis puts it: "Lord, grant that I may not so much seek to . . . be loved as to love; for it is in giving that we receive. . . ." This paradox goes back to Jesus himself, who tells us that those who are willing to lose their life for his sake will find it (Matthew 16:25). To a world that often confuses narcissism with true love, Bernard speaks of a generous and selfless love, charged with the presence and power of God, that will satisfy our deepest longings.

Chapter 5

Union with God

We now come to Bernard's literary masterpiece, his eighty-six *Sermons on the Song of Songs*. Here Bernard recounts in great detail the process of becoming united with God in love. This is where Bernard's mysticism—his experience of intimacy with God—shines forth most radiantly.

These sermons can be simultaneously the most delightful and the most frustrating of Bernard's works to read. On the one hand, they are overflowing with enthusiasm, creativity, and spiritual insight. On the other hand, they often interpret scripture passages in ways that can only be described as outlandish, and (as we have seen in other works by Bernard) they sometimes wander off into long digressions that seem to have little to do with their main subject.

Bernard began writing these sermons in 1135 and continued to work on them until his death in 1153. He wrote eighty-six sermons and only made it to the beginning of the third chapter of the Song. It ended up taking two other monks to finish the work that Bernard had begun.

Modern-day scripture scholars generally see the Song of Songs as a love poem, or a collection of love poems, that describes an intimate relationship between a man and a woman. This "literal" interpretation of the Song is fairly recent. For most of its history, the Song of Songs has been interpreted as an allegory of the love relationship between God and God's people, taken to be Israel by Jewish readers, and the church by Christian readers.

Indeed, there is a general consensus that the Song would not have made it into the canon of scripture had it been understood to refer simply to a love shared between two human beings. The Song certainly expresses human love in its highest manifestations, and many commentators read Song 8:6 as a statement that human love is a spark of the divine. But it is important to recognize that traditional interpretations of the Song have not proceeded along these lines.

Bernard takes as a given the allegorical character of the Song of Songs. On several occasions he explictly rejects a "physical" interpretation of the Song as illegitimate and unworthy of the spiritual nature of the text. For example, in reflecting on the significance of the beloved leaping over mountains and hills in Song 2:8, Bernard asks:

Shall we imagine for ourselves a powerful man of great stature, captivated by the love of an absent girl-friend and hastening to her desired embraces by bounding over these mountains and hills whose massive bulk we see towering to such heights above the plain that the peaks of some seem to penetrate the clouds? Surely it will not do to fabricate physical images of this kind, especially when treating of this spiritual Song; and it is certainly not legitimate for us who recall reading in the Gospel that "God is a spirit and those who worship him must worship in spirit." (SC 53.3)

Similarly, he rejects a literal interpretation of "catching the little foxes" in Song 2:15: "We must totally reject in our interpretation the common and familiar meaning of the text as absurd and insipid and clearly unworthy of inclusion in holy and authentic scripture" (SC 63.1).

This does not mean that Bernard's interpretation of the Song is going to be boring and dry—far from it! Bernard uses vivid imagery and provocative, even erotic, language, in describing the spiritual marriage between God and the soul. At times, a single word in the text will evoke a reflection that continues through several sermons. It becomes obvious in reading the sermons that these are exquisitely constructed literary works and not sermons that were delivered orally in their present form.

In the commentary that follows, I will present some of the highlights of Bernard's sermons on the Song, with an emphasis on how these sermons can speak to Christians today. It should be noted that Bernard himself did not address these sermons to "people in the world" but to his monks (see SC 1.1). Just as in his other "monastic" writings, however, there are riches here that can be mined by any person of faith.

To a greater degree than most of his other works, Bernard's *Sermons on the Song of Songs* emphasize the importance of personal experience. One often gets the sense of self-disclosure in these sermons, even in places where Bernard does not explicitly make reference to himself. As he says in Sermon 1:

Only the touch of the Spirit can inspire a song like this, and only personal experience can unfold its meaning. Let those who are versed in the mystery revel in it; *let all others burn with desire rather to attain to this experience than merely to learn about it.* For it is not a melody that resounds abroad but the very music of the heart, not a trilling on the lips but an inward pulsing of delight, a harmony not of voices but of wills. (SC 1.11, emphasis added)

We have already seen that for Bernard, and indeed for monasticism in general, all knowledge of God was meant to lead to greater love and devotion. Thus, Bernard's goal is not simply to teach us *about* union with God but to show us how we can come to experience it. In the process, he offers insights into several other areas of Christian life.

The Foundation of Mystical Union

As we have seen in his other writings, Bernard sees the path to union with God as a process, grounded in and propelled by the power of God's grace. In the earliest sermons, Bernard reminds his readers of the journey they must first make from sin to righteousness, and how this is rooted in the love of Christ and the power of the Holy Spirit.

Bernard begins his reflection on the Song of Songs with the verse, "Let him kiss me with the kiss of his mouth" (Song 1:2). What is this kiss? Bernard later refers to it as the gift of the Holy Spirit (SC 8.2). From whose mouth comes the kiss? There can be only one answer: from Jesus, who mediates God's love and grace to us:

The mouth that kisses signifies the Word who assumes human nature; the nature assumed receives the kiss; the kiss however, that takes its being both from the giver and the receiver, is a person that is formed by both, none other than "the one mediator between God and mankind, himself a man, Christ Jesus." It is for this reason that none of the saints dared say: "let him kiss me with his mouth," but rather, "with the kiss of his mouth." In this way they paid tribute to that prerogative of Christ, on whom uniquely and in one sole instance the mouth of the Word was pressed, that moment when the fullness of the divinity yielded itself to him as the life of his body. (SC 2.3)

We can identify the "kiss on the mouth" with contemplation or mystical union. It is the experience of being totally centered on God, of being one with God in love. At the beginning of Sermon 3, Bernard invites his readers to study "the book of our own experience" (SC 3.1) and asks whether we have been privileged to say, "Let him kiss me with the kiss of his mouth." He goes on to make a very important statement:

Those to whom it is given to utter these words sincerely are comparatively few, but any one who has received this mystical kiss from the mouth of Christ at least once, seeks again that intimate experience, and eagerly looks for its frequent renewal. I think that nobody can grasp what it is except the one who receives it. . . . But a soul like mine, burdened with sins, still subject to carnal passions, devoid of any knowledge of spiritual delights, may not presume to make such a request, almost totally unacquainted as it is with the joys of the supernatural life. (SC 3.1)

It seems as if Bernard is suggesting here that he has not had the experience of contemplation himself. Later in the sermons, he will admit that he has. His point, though, is to emphasize that none of us begins with a kiss on the mouth, but that we only come to this after we have first approached Jesus for forgiveness, repented of our sins, and persevered in living the spiritual life—all of which is seen as being entirely dependent on God's grace. Bernard will speak of these stages using the metaphors of kissing the feet, the hands, and finally the mouth of Jesus:

There is first the forgiveness of sins [kissing the feet of Jesus], then the grace that follows on good deeds [kissing the hand of Jesus], and finally that contemplative gift by which a kind and beneficent Lord shows himself to the soul with as much clarity as bodily frailty can endure [kissing the mouth of Jesus]. (SC 4.1)

Bernard is well aware that he is speaking metaphorically here. God does not literally have feet, hands, and a mouth, for God is spirit. Bernard states,

I allow of course that God does not have these members by his nature, they represent certain modes of our encounter with him. The heartfelt desire to admit one's guilt brings a man down in lowliness before God, as it were to his feet; the heartfelt devotion of a worshiper finds in God renewal and refreshment, the touch, as it were, of his hand; and the delights of contemplation lead on to that ecstatic repose that is the fruit of the kiss of his mouth. (SC 4.4)

It was precisely because of God's immateriality, however, that his work among human beings in ancient times was "hidden" or "shrouded." People failed to understand God's presence and power, attributing God's accomplishments to their own human efforts. But God did not leave people in their ignorance and sin:

God had mercy on their errors: coming forth from his shady and thickly covered mountain, he pitched his tent in the sun. He became incarnate for the sake of carnal men, that he might induce them to relish the life of the Spirit. In the body and through the body he performed works of which not man but God was the author. . . . In the body, I repeat, and through the body, he performed wonderful deeds with an authority that was obvious. He proclaimed the message of salvation and endured outrage, thus clearly demonstrating that he it was whose invisible power created the world, whose wisdom governed it, and whose benevolence protected it. (SC 6.3).

For Bernard, the significance of the Incarnation cannot be overstated, as we will see in more detail presently. It is precisely through devotion to the humanity of Jesus that we will progress to the higher spiritual devotion that leads to contemplation.

Having spoken at some length about Jesus, Bernard turns his attention to the Spirit. In Sermon 8 he defines the kiss of the mouth as the gift of the Holy Spirit (SC 8.2). Bernard understands the Spirit as the "love and benign goodness" of the Father and the Son (SC 8.4). It is the Holy Spirit who inspires us not just to *know* God but to *love and honor* God. Indeed, it is the Spirit who makes it possible for us to participate in the relationship of love between the Father and the Son.

Bernard insists that only Jesus receives the Father's kiss directly:

He however who did not count equality with God a thing to be grasped, since he could dare to say: "The Father and I are one," because he was joined to him as an equal and embraced him as an equal—he does not beg for a kiss from an inferior position; rather on equally sublime heights mouth is joined to mouth, and by a prerogative that is unique he receives the kiss from the mouth. For Christ therefore, the kiss meant a totality, for Paul only a participation; Christ rejoiced in the kiss of the mouth, Paul only in that he was kissed by the kiss. (SC 8.8)

For Bernard, the awkward phrase about being "kissed by the kiss" is the Song's way of reminding us that our experience of union with God is mediated—we "participate" in this relationship of love but are not totally absorbed in it as the persons of the Trinity are. Still, this participation, which takes place through the power of the Holy Spirit, is no small thing:

Felicitous, however, is this kiss of participation that enables us not only to know God but to love the Father, who is never fully known until he is perfectly loved. . . . Let that man who feels he is moved by the same Spirit as the Son, let him know that he too is loved by the Father. . . . For if marriage according to the flesh constitutes two in one body, why should not a spiritual union be even more efficacious in joining two in one spirit? And hence anyone who is joined to the Lord is one spirit with him. (SC 8.9)

This last sentence is a reference to 1 Corinthians 6:17. It is one of Bernard's favorite passages and epitomizes for him the meaning of mystical union. It is a spiritual union, a union in love, and not a union of identity or essence.

Also worth noting in this passage is Bernard's belief that God is not really known until he is loved. Earlier in this sermon, Bernard reflects on Romans 1:21, where Paul speaks of people who claimed to know God but refused to honor him:

We do not read that they knew by a revelation of the Holy Spirit; for even though they possessed knowledge, they did not love. . . . They were content with the knowledge that gives self-importance, but ignorant of the love that makes the building grow. . . . For if their knowledge had been complete, they would not have been blind to that goodness by which he willed to be born a human being, and to die for their sins. (SC 8.5)

Throughout the sermons, Bernard sometimes refers to the church as the bride and to God as the bridegroom, but most often he speaks of the believer as the bride and specifically of Jesus as the bridegroom. He summarizes the words of the bride up to this point:

"I cannot rest," she said, "unless he kisses me with the kiss of his mouth. I thank him for the kiss of the feet, I thank him too for the kiss of the hand; but if he has genuine regard for me, let him kiss me with the kiss of his mouth. There is no question of ingratitude on my part, it is simply that I am in love. The favors I have received are far above what I deserve, but they are less than what I long for. *It is desire that drives me on,* not reason. Please do not accuse me of presumption if I yield to this impulse of love. . . ." (SC 9.2, emphasis added)

The quest for contemplation is driven by desire. This is a strong theme in the sermons, and it corresponds to one of the most central qualities of monastic life that we saw in chapter 1, the desire for God.

At this point the reader should note that Bernard has already written eight full sermons, and he has only commented on one verse of the Song! Clearly, Bernard sees each verse of this text as bursting with meaning. It is no wonder that he never finished the sermons. It is important to grasp something of the meticulous detail with which Bernard concerned himself in writing the sermons, and to illustrate this I have reviewed Sermons 1–8 in some detail. Even so, I have only scratched the surface of what Bernard has written here. A careful reading of the sermons in their entirety will yield rich rewards.

In the middle of Sermon 9, Bernard finally moves on to Song 1:3, which in the Vulgate (Bernard's Latin Bible) reads, "For your breasts are better than wine, smelling sweet of the best ointments." Bernard will spend several sermons expounding the meaning of this text. He speaks in Sermon 10 of three ointments that adorn the breasts: contrition (sorrow for sin), devotion (thankfulness for God's goodness), and piety (acts of loving kindness). First, Bernard turns again to the reality of our status as sinners, as he did in his exposition of kissing the feet of Jesus. But he hastens to point out that we should not dwell on our sinfulness:

Sorrow for sin is indeed necessary, but it should not be an endless preoccupation. You must dwell also on the glad remembrance of God's loving-kindness, otherwise sadness will harden the heart and lead it more deeply into despair. . . . Hence the just man is not always accusing himself, he does so only in the opening words of his intercourse with God; he will normally conclude that intercourse with the divine praises. (SC 11.2)

We should especially thank God for the gift of redemption (SC 11.3), which makes all intimacy with God possible.

The third ointment is called piety or "the grace of loving-kindness." He gives it this name

because the elements that go into its making are the needs of the poor, the anxieties of the oppressed, the worries of those who are sad, the sins of wrong-doers, and finally, the manifold misfortunes of people of all classes who endure affliction, even if they are our enemies. (SC 12.1)

Bernard proceeds to review the kindness and generosity of several biblical figures, including St. Paul, Job, Joseph (the son of the patriarch Jacob), and Moses. He then makes the connection to his readers:

A similar influence is achieved by those too who, in the course of this life have been indulgent and charitable, who have made an effort to show kindness to their fellow-men, not vindicating to themselves alone any grace they were gifted with, but exercising it for the common good in the consciousness that they owe a duty to enemies no less than friends, to the wise just as much as to the unwise. . . . [E]veryone, I repeat, who performs such deeds among you, gives forth a good odor among the brethren like a rare and delicate perfume. (SC 12.5)

Bernard repeatedly refers to the superiority of this ointment over the others. This is significant, because what it shows is that Bernard places a very high value on our becoming loving servants of God and of one another. Indeed, in the end, Bernard will say that this is more important than the experience of contemplation, as we will see more clearly below.

Bernard is well aware of the difficulty of living up to these ideals, expressed in the three ointments. He asks,

Which of us can live uprightly and perfectly even for one hour, an hour free from fruitless talk and careless work? Yet there is one who truthfully and unhesitatingly can glory in this praise. She is the Church. . . . With the bold assurance of one confident that her breasts are better than wine and redolent of the choicest perfumes, she lays claim to the title of bride. And although none of us will dare arrogate for his own soul the title of bride of the Lord, nevertheless we are members of the Church which rightly boasts of this title and of the reality that it signifies, and hence may justifiably assume a share in this honor. (SC 12.11)

It is important to notice here that for Bernard, our relationship with God grows and develops in the context of our membership in the church, the community of faith. It is the church that is the primary referent of the title of Bride. Thus even contemplation, as personal an experience as it is, is not a private experience but has an inherently ecclesial dimension.

One final foundational point must be mentioned: our union with God, though it is fulfilled in the realm of the spiritual, begins through our love of the humanity of Jesus

Christ. Bernard develops this point with particular directness in Sermon 20. He states:

Notice that the love of the heart is, in a certain sense, carnal, because our hearts are attracted most toward the humanity of Christ and the things he did or commanded while in the flesh. . . . I think this is the principal reason why the invisible God willed to be seen in the flesh and to converse with men as a man. He wanted to recapture the affections of carnal men who were unable to love in any other way, by first drawing them to the salutary love of his own humanity, and then gradually to raise them to a spiritual love. (SC 20.6)

This "carnal love," Bernard goes on to say, "becomes better when it is rational, and becomes perfect when it is spiritual" (SC 20.9). This movement takes place through the power of the Holy Spirit.

Thus, Bernard begins his sermons on contemplation by reviewing several basic themes of Christian faith, especially the forgiveness of sin, the centrality of Jesus Christ and the Holy Spirit, the indispensability of the church, and the importance of a life of Christian service. Bernard will never forget these things as he describes the road to contemplation. That road is fueled by an insatiable desire for God, itself a gift of the Holy Spirit, which begins with a love of Jesus's humanity and progresses to a spiritual love.

The Nature of Mystical Union

Bernard does not seem to have had a systematic plan in his mind when he wrote the *Sermons on the Song of Songs*. This is probably already clear from the description of the earliest sermons above. However, certain basic themes do emerge. I think it would be most helpful to continue our study of the *Sermons* by focusing on these.

(a) The Primacy of God's Love (Grace)

There is no question that love is the central theme of the *Sermons*. Bernard alternates between discussing God's love for the soul and the soul's love for God. Bernard refers again and again, however, to the primacy of God's love. God's love is always the condition of and the power behind our own:

> When the Word therefore tells the soul, "You are beautiful," and calls it friend, he infuses into it the power to love, and to know it is loved in return. And when the soul addresses him as beloved and praises his beauty, she is filled with admiration for his goodness and attributes to him without subterfuge or deceit the grace by which she loves and is loved. The Bridegroom's beauty is his love of the bride, all the greater in that it existed before hers. Realizing then that he was her lover before he was her beloved, she cries out with strength and ardor that she must love him with her whole heart and with words expressing deepest affection. The speech of the Word is an infusion of grace, the soul's response is wonder and thanksgiving. The more she feels surpassed in her loving the more she gives in love; and her wonder grows when he still exceeds her. (SC 45.8)

This rich passage is reminiscent of what we have seen in other writings of Bernard, that everything is rooted in grace. For Bernard, divine love triggers a process that makes its recipient want to love God as much as possible in return. Bernard is emphatic that our love is totally dependent on God's:

> Do you keep watch? He keeps watch also. If you rise at night before the time of vigil and hasten to anticipate the

morning watch, you will find him there. He will always be waiting for you. You would be very rash if you claimed to love him first or love him more; his love is greater, and it preceded yours. (SC 69.8)

Indeed, Bernard will often insist that only those who give proper glory to God for his gifts will be led to experience contemplation.

At times, Bernard speaks of our own good works as preceding the "marriage bed" of contemplation. In Sermon 46, he states:

You must take care to surround [your marriage bed] with the flowers of good works, with the practice of virtues, that precede holy contemplation as the flower precedes the fruit. Otherwise, instead of seeking rest after labor you will want to slumber on in luxurious ease. . . . But it is a perversion of order to demand the reward before it is earned, to take food and not to work. (SC 46.5)

This may sound as if Bernard thinks that our good works somehow "merit" contemplation. But as we have seen elsewhere, Bernard thinks that our good works are themselves gifts from God and that we can claim no merits for ourselves. Bernard is absolutely convinced that the contemplative experience begins and ends with grace:

With exquisite subtlety, [the Bride] follows the order of the Prophet and says: "I am my Beloved's and he is mine." Why this? Surely that she may show herself more full of grace when she surrenders wholly to grace, attributing to him both the beginning and the ending. How indeed could she be full of grace if there were any part of her which did not itself spring from grace? There is no way for grace to enter, if [a sense of] merit has taken residence in the soul. . . . I want nothing to do with the sort of merit which excludes grace. (SC 67.10)

(b) A Union of Spirits

We saw in chapter 4 that Bernard sees the highest degree of love as a union of wills. Thus he will not speak of the "absorption" of the soul into God, or of a union of essences, but rather of an intimate *relationship* between the contemplative and God. Bernard develops this idea extensively in the *Sermons on the Song of Songs*.

In Sermon 62, Bernard reflects on the difference between scrutinizing God's majesty and scrutinizing God's will:

Scrutinizing God's majesty is then a thing to fear; but scrutinizing his will is as safe as it is dutiful. Why should I not tirelessly concentrate on searching into the mystery of his glorious will, which I know I must obey in all things? . . . We are transformed when we are conformed. God forbid that a man presume to be conformed to God in the glory of his majesty rather than in the modesty of his will. (SC 62.5)

Bernard does say that it is appropriate to *admire* God's majesty (SC 62.4), but we can never share in it, for that would be tantamount to an essential union. Conformity to God's will brings us as close as we will get to God, and that is very close indeed.

Again and again, Bernard speaks of the union between the Word and the soul as a spiritual union. He often refers to 1 Corinthians 6:17, one of his favorite passages in scripture, in expounding this point:

Be careful, however, not to conclude that I see something corporeal or perceptible to the senses in this union between the Word and the soul. My opinion is that of the Apostle, who said that "he who is united to the Lord becomes one spirit with him" [1 Corinthians 6:17]. I try to express with the most suitable words I can muster the ecstatic ascent of the purified mind to God, and the loving descent of God into the soul, submitting spiritual truths to spiritual men. Therefore let this union be in the spirit, because "God is a spirit" [John 4:24], who is lovingly drawn by the beauty of that soul whom he perceives to be guided by the Spirit, and devoid of any desire to submit to the ways of the flesh, especially if he sees that it burns with love for himself. (SC 31.6)

Perhaps the clearest statement of Bernard's thinking on this point is found in Sermon 71. Bernard contrasts the unity that exists within the Trinity with the unity that we can have with God:

The Father and the Son cannot be said to be one person, because the Father is one and the Son is one. Yet they are said to be, and they are, one, because they have and are one substance, since they have not each separate substance. On the contrary, since God and man do not share the same nature or substance, they cannot be said to be a unity, yet they are with complete truth and accuracy, said to be one spirit, if they cohere with the bond of love. But that unity is caused not so much by the identity of essences as by the concurrence of wills. (SC 71.8)

Bernard also relates this theme to that of the spiritual marriage, as we shall see below.

(c) A Union that Is Mutual, Not Equal

Bernard speaks so glowingly of the love between God and the soul that we may get the impression that he is talking about a relationship between equals. However, a careful reading of Bernard will reveal that this is not his intent. Bernard does sometimes speak of an intimate "friendship" between the bridegroom and the bride (e.g., in SC 43.1), but this does not mean that the soul is God's equal. Rather,

God, whose majesty is absolute, condescends in an act of great humility to share an experience of love with the bride. In speaking of this, Bernard can barely restrain his enthusiasm:

I cannot restrain my joy that this majesty did not disdain to bend down to our weakness in a companionship so familiar and sweet, that the supreme Godhead did not scorn to enter into wedlock with the soul in exile and to reveal to her with the most ardent love how affectionate was this bridegroom whom she had won. (SC 52.2)

Later, commenting on Song 2:16, Bernard speaks candidly about the inequality of the love relationship:

"My beloved is mine and I am his." There is no doubt that in this passage a shared love blazes up, but a love in which one of them experiences the highest felicity, while the other shows marvellous condescension. There is no betrothal or union of equals here. (SC 67.8)

In the very next sermon, continuing to marvel over this relationship, he exclaims, "But how unequal a partnership!" (SC 68.1).

Although our union with God is not a union of equals, Bernard does describe it as perfectly *mutual*. In Sermon 83, speaking of the inexhaustible fountain of God's love, he writes:

Although the creature loves less, being a lesser being, yet if it loves with its whole heart nothing is lacking, for it has given all. Such love, as I have said, is marriage, for a soul cannot love like this and not be beloved; complete and perfect marriage consists in the exchange of love. No one can doubt that the soul is first loved, and loved more intensely, by the Word; for it is anticipated and surpassed in its love. Happy the soul who is permitted to be anticipated in blessedness so sweet! Happy the soul who has been allowed to experience the embrace of such bliss! For it is nothing other than love, holy and chaste, full of sweetness and delight, love utterly serene and true, *mutual* and deep, which joins two beings, not in one flesh, but in one spirit, making them no longer two but one. (SC 83.6, emphasis added)

Again, notice here how emphatic Bernard is about God's love being prior to ours, more intense, and surpassing.

(d) A Rare, Incomplete, and Fleeting Experience

In the treatise *On Loving God*, we encountered Bernard's belief that the highest stage of love is rarely experienced in this life. He speaks in a similar fashion in the *Sermons on the Song of Songs*. First, we should note that even the contemplative does not really see God "as he is":

Those who contemplate him without ceasing are short of nothing, those whose wills are fixed on him have nothing more to desire.

But this vision is not for the present life; it is reserved for the next, at least for those who can say: "We know that when he appears we shall be like him, for we shall see him as he is" [1 John 3:2]. Even now he appears to whom he pleases, but as he pleases, not as he is. Neither sage nor saint nor prophet can or could ever see him as he is, while still in this mortal body; but whoever is found worthy will be able to do so when the body becomes immortal. Hence, though he is seen here below, it is in the form that seems good to him, not as he is. For example, take that mighty source of light, I speak of that sun which you see day after day; yet you do not see it as it is, but according as it lights up the air, or a mountain, or a wall. (SC 31.1-2)

However, Bernard goes on to say that "in this inward vision [God] does not reveal himself as altogether different from what he is" either (SC 31.7). In other words, the contemplative experience is an authentic experience of divine love. Bernard believes that God accommodates himself to our capacities:

But you, if you love the Lord your God with your whole heart, whole mind, whole strength, and leaping with ardent feeling beyond that love of love with which active love is satisfied and having received the Spirit in fullness, are wholly aflame with that divine love to which the former is a step, then God is indeed experienced, although not as he truly is, a thing impossible for any creature, but rather in relation to your power to enjoy. (SC 50.6)

We will have more to say below about the "active" love that Bernard mentions here.

Those who do enjoy an experience of loving union find that it is a fleeting one. Bernard has had the experience himself, and he speaks about it on a few occasions in the sermons. In Sermon 23, he says:

But there is a place where God is seen in tranquil rest, where he is neither Judge nor Teacher but Bridegroom. To me—for I do not speak for others—this is truly the bedroom to which I have sometimes gained happy entrance. Alas! how rare the time, and how short the stay! (SC 23.15)

In Sermon 74, Bernard reflects at greater length on his own contemplative experiences. In this context, he stresses the mysterious nature of the encounters:

I admit that the Word has also come to me—I speak as a fool—and has come many times. But although he has come to me, I have never been conscious of the moment of his coming. I perceived his presence, I remembered afterwards that he had been with me; sometimes I had a presentiment that he would come, but I was never conscious of his coming or his going. And where he comes from when he visits my soul, and where he goes, and by what means he enters and goes out, I admit that I do not know even now; as John says, "You do not know where he comes from or where he goes" [John 3:8]. (SC 74.5)

How then did Bernard recognize that he was being visited by God? He knew it because of the effect of the visitation: a profound sense of peace, satisfied desire, and awe:

It was not by any movement of his that I recognized his coming; it was not by any of my senses that I perceived he had penetrated to the depths of my being. Only by the movement of my heart, as I have told you, did I perceive his presence; and I knew the power of his might because my faults were put to flight and my human yearnings brought into subjection. I have marvelled at the depth of his wisdom when my secret faults have been revealed and made visible; at the very slightest amendment of my way of life I have experienced his goodness and mercy; in the renewal and remaking of the spirit of my mind, that is of my inmost being, I have perceived the excellence of his glorious beauty, and when I contemplate all these things I am filled with awe and wonder at his manifold greatness. (SC 74.6)

Bernard speaks of the happiness that accompanies this experience as "a happiness that is never complete because the joy of the visit is followed by the pain at his departure" (SC 32.2). Indeed, as we saw earlier in a quotation from Sermon 3, the person who has received this mystical kiss from Christ "seeks again that intimate experience, and eagerly looks for its frequent renewal" (SC 3.1).

What about those who have never had such an experience of union? Bernard's answer is that all people, whether or not they experience contemplation, are saved by grace through faith, and not through mystical visions. In Sermon 84, Bernard says, "Let those who do not have such an experience [of contemplation] believe, so that by the merit of their faith they will reap the fruit of experience" (SC 84.7, translation mine).

This will come as a great consolation to those of us who have not had such intense spiritual experiences, not even fleetingly. Although Bernard does not say that any Christian is excluded from contemplative experience, he does not seem to think that contemplation will happen for everyone; in fact, he believes that this kind of experience is most likely to take place within the monastery.

Even those who do experience contemplation will find that it takes up a very small part of their Christian life. This brings us to a consideration of how Bernard sees contemplation in relation to the active life of a Christian.

(e) The Complementarity of Contemplation and Action

One of the distinctions that Bernard makes in these sermons is between "active" and "affective" love. As he says in Sermon 50, "Love exists in action and in feeling" (SC 50.2), by which he means to distinguish our love of God from our love of our neighbors. Bernard does not hesitate to say that affective love, which is involved in contemplation, is to be more highly valued than active love:

Now the active prefers what is lowly, the affective what is lofty. For example, there is no doubt that in a mind that loves rightly, the love of God is valued more than love of men, and among men themselves the more perfect [is esteemed] more than the weaker, heaven more than earth, eternity more than the flesh. (SC 50.5)

However, Bernard immediately qualifies this statement, declaring that active love usually, if not always, must take precedence:

In well-regulated action, on the other hand, the opposite order frequently or even always prevails. For we are more strongly impelled toward and more often occupied with the welfare of our neighbor; we attend our weaker brothers with more exacting care; by human right and very necessity we concentrate more on peace on earth than on the glory of heaven; by worrying about temporal cares we are not permitted to think of eternal things; in attending almost continually to the ills of our body we lay aside the care of our soul; and finally, in accord with the saying of the Apostle, we invest our weaker members with greater honor, so fulfilling in a sense the word of the Lord: "the last shall be first and the first last." Who will doubt that in prayer a man is speaking with God? But how often, at the call of charity, we are drawn away, torn away, for the sake of those who need to speak to us or be helped! How often does dutiful repose yield dutifully to the uproar of business! . . . A preposterous order; but necessity knows no law. (SC 50.5)

Bernard concludes that "true love is found in this, that those whose need is greater receive first" (SC 50.6).

In other words, Bernard recognizes that for most people most of the time, our love must be expressed in active service. He knew this himself, as his busy schedule both in and out of the monastery made it difficult to find time for his own life of prayer. In Sermon 52 he comments on being "intruded upon" by his monks: "Let me not seek my own advantage; it is what is useful not to me but to many that I shall judge useful to myself" (SC 52.7). So, although Bernard speaks highly of a life of contemplative solitude, he realizes that it is a rare person indeed who can enjoy this privilege.

This is not to say that Bernard sees the active and contemplative life in competition with each other. Rather, he sees active love as a "step" to affective love. Bernard will insist on the complementarity of the two kinds of love. The person who is active in service will be a better contemplative, and vice versa, as these excerpts from two of his sermons show:

After a good work one rests more securely in contemplation, and the more a man is conscious that he has not failed in works of charity through love of his own ease, the more faithfully will he contemplate things sublime and make bold to study them. (SC 47.4)

It is characteristic of true and pure contemplation that when the mind is ardently aglow with God's love, it is sometimes so filled with zeal and the desire to gather to God those who will love him with equal abandon that it gladly forgoes contemplative leisure for the endeavor of preaching. (SC 57.9)

In another sermon, he speaks of action and contemplation as "comrades" who live together, "for Martha is sister to Mary" (SC 51.2). This reference connects Bernard to a longstanding tradition of seeing Martha as a model of the active life and Mary as a model of the contemplative.

(f) A Spiritual Marriage

Although Bernard admits that contemplation is a rare and fleeting experience and that it is not more important than faith, or in practical reality than action, nevertheless he delights that some are privileged to share in it. In describing the nature of the experience, he returns again and again to the image of a spiritual marriage. This image is presented with particular directness and eloquence in Sermon 83:

When she loves perfectly, the soul is wedded to the Word. What is lovelier than this conformity? What is more desirable than charity, by whose operation, O soul, not content with a human master, you approach the Word with confidence, cling to him with constancy, speak to him as to a familiar friend, and refer to him in every matter with an intellectual grasp proportionate to the boldness of your desire? Truly this is a spiritual contract, a holy marriage. It is more than a contract, it is an embrace: an embrace where identity of will makes of two one spirit. (SC 83.3)

The relationship between the bride and the bridegroom is characterized above all by love, for Bernard sees love as the only one of our affections that is similar enough to God that there can be a mutual relationship:

Love is the only one of the motions of the soul, of its senses and affections, in which the creature can respond to its Creator, even if not as an equal, and repay his favor in some similar way. For example, if God is angry with me, am I to be angry in return? No, indeed, but I shall tremble with fear and ask pardon. So also, if he accuses me, I shall not accuse him in return, but rather justify him. Nor, if he judges me, shall I judge him, but I shall adore him; and in saving me he does not asked to be saved by me; nor does he who sets all men free, need to be set free by me. If he commands, I must obey, and not demand his service or obedience. Now you see how different love is, for when God loves, he desires nothing but to be loved, since he loves us for no other reason than to be loved, for he knows that those who love him are blessed in their very love. (SC 83.4)

The last verse of the Song that Bernard gets to comment on is Song 3:1, "Nightlong in my little bed I sought him whom my soul loves." Having spoken of the joys of the spiritual marriage, Bernard comes full circle and returns to the point he made when he started writing the sermons:

everything is the result of grace. He begins Sermon 84 with a quotation from Psalm 104:4, which speaks of seeking God's face always. He continues:

Now I see why I have begun this way. Surely so that every soul among you who is seeking God may know that she has been forestalled, and that she was found before she was sought. This will avoid distorting her greatest good into a great evil; for this is what we do when we receive favors from God and treat his gifts as though they were ours by right, and do not give glory to God. (SC 84.2)

Bernard repeats this point over and over again in the sermon. And it is a powerful point, a central one in Bernard's teaching. The most important thing in a Christian's life is the desire for God, and that desire is itself a gift from God.

The Significance of the Sermons

The topic of mystical union is not one to which most people can easily relate. As we have seen in this brief review of some of the central themes in Bernard's *Sermons on the Song of Songs*, contemplation entails a sublime and mysterious type of experience that most of us would hesitate to claim we have had.

Nevertheless, these sermons touch on several themes that are important in any Christian's life of faith: rejoicing in God's grace and particularly in God's love, recognizing the importance of Jesus's humanity in bringing us to experience God's love, seeking to love God—which entails conforming ourselves to God's will—to the greatest extent possible in our lives, and recognizing that love of God impels us to love our neighbors and serve their needs.

At the same time, we should not be too quick to dismiss

the possibility of a contemplative experience. Maybe, in our obsessively active world, if we all take more time out to pray and to be attentive to the movement of God's spirit in our lives, we will find ourselves feasting on some of the spiritual delights of which Bernard speaks so eloquently. Contemplative experience may be just a brief and imperfect foretaste of what awaits us in heaven, but it can renew our spirit and give us strength for the challenging task of witnessing to God's love for the world.

Chapter 6

Spirituality and Leadership

Bernard's exquisite reflections on the Song of Songs make it clear that there was nothing more important to him than the pursuit of spiritual union with God. However, we saw that even in writing about the delights of contemplation, Bernard was not unaware of the realities and demands of ordinary existence. He recognized that contemplation and action are both essential elements of the spiritual life and, indeed, complement one another. To put it in more contemporary language, he was quite interested in the integration of the spiritual and the practical.

Bernard expressed this concern with particular clarity in his *Five Books on Consideration*, a series of writings addressed to Pope Eugene III. Eugene, as the leader of the Christian world, had to deal with the tension between spirituality and worldly responsibility to a degree that, in Bernard's view, was unique among Christians. So Bernard took it upon himself to give him some advice. The result is a treatise on spiritual government that has much to say not only to church leaders but to all Christians who are striving to integrate the spiritual and the practical in their lives. It is fitting, therefore, that we end our review of Bernard's writings with this work.

What gave Bernard the audacity to presume to give

advice to the pope? Aside from the fact that Bernard was already used to being a consultant to high church officials, Eugene, who became pope in 1145, had been one of Bernard's monks at Clairvaux. It should be noted that Bernard was not especially thrilled with Eugene's election. Bernard sent a letter to the Roman Curia expressing his disappointment:

Had you no other wise and experienced man amongst you who would have been better suited for these things? It certainly seems ridiculous to take a man in rags and make him preside over princes, command bishops, and dispose of kingdoms and empires. Ridiculous or miraculous? Either one or the other. (LB 315.2)

Bernard went on to concede that this "could be the work of God," especially since so many others had taken it to be so. But this did not calm his reservations:

I am not happy in my own mind [with Eugene's election], for his nature is delicate, and his tender diffidence is more accustomed to leisure than to dealing in great affairs. I fear that he might not exercise his apostolate with sufficient firmness. What do you think will be the feelings of a man who from the secrets of contemplation and the sweet solitude of his heart, suddenly finds himself plunged into a vortex of great affairs, like a child suddenly snatched from his mother's arms, like a sheep being led to sacrifice and finding itself in unfamiliar and unwelcome surroundings? (LB 315.3)

In short, Bernard was not happy with the idea of any monk being taken from his monastery to attend to church administration, and he was particularly concerned that Eugene might not be up to the task, given his frail constitution. He begged the cardinals and bishops of the curia to give Eugene the assistance that he needed to fulfill his role as pontiff:

Unless the Lord support him with his hand, he must necessarily be overcome and crushed under such an excessive and unaccustomed load, formidable even for a giant, even for the very angels themselves. Nevertheless because it has been done, and many are saying it has been done by the Lord, it must be your concern, dearest friends, to help and comfort with your fervent support what is clearly the work of your hands. If you have in you any power to console, if there is in you any charity from the Lord, if you have any pity, any compassion, support him in the work to which he has been lifted up by the Lord through you. (LB 315.3)

But Bernard was not about to leave well enough alone. In addition to exhorting the cardinals and bishops, he was himself determined to continue to be a mentor to Eugene. Thus the *Five Books on Consideration* were born. Bernard wrote the treatise starting around 1148 and completed it just before his own death in 1153.

Eugene's basic dilemma is well summarized by translator Elizabeth Kennan:

As a Cistercian, Eugene was dedicated to the perfection of his own spiritual life. His being was centered in prayer, in study and in contemplation of God. But as pope, Eugene was responsible for the administration of the Curia, the regulation of the hierarchy, the protection of monasteries, the safety of the Holy Land, the morality of the powerful, the health and well-being of the widowed and orphaned, and, not least, the reconquest of Rome. That work load made the New Jerusalem look like a mirage. (DC, introduction, p. 16)

Bernard's basic message to Eugene is that he needs to seek a balance by following a middle course in all of the situations where this tension is manifest.

The first two books of the treatise focus for the most part on the pope himself. Bernard defines "consideration" and speaks of how Eugene needs to apply it to his life. Books three to five then speak of the milieu in which Eugene finds himself: those who are below him (his subjects), those who are around him (his household and immediate environment), and those who are above him (angels and God). So, the treatise concludes on an exalted note. Indeed, we shall see that Bernard returns in the end to his most cherished theme, the search for God. Let us now take a closer look at each book in the treatise, and see what insights it holds for Christians and Christian leaders today.

Book One: Papal Challenges and Consideration

Bernard begins by focusing on the burdens of the papal office, specifically Eugene's crowded calendar of appointments. He fears that getting caught up in these could lead to hardness of heart. Bernard singles out litigation as a particular curse of the papal office, especially when it involves people who are seeking only financial or political gain:

What is more servile and more unworthy, especially for the Supreme Pontiff, than every day, or rather every hour, to sweat over such affairs for the likes of these [people seeking their own gain]? Tell me this, when are we to pray or to teach the people? When are we to build up the Church or meditate on the law? (DC 1.5)

Again and again in this treatise, Bernard hammers away at the idea that the pope is called to *spiritual* leadership, not engagement in disputes over worldly matters. He goes on to say:

Clearly your power is over sin and not property, since it is because of sin that you have received the keys of the heavenly kingdom, to exclude sinners not possessors. The Lord confirms this when he says, "That you may know that the Son of Man has power on earth to forgive sins." Tell me, which seems to you the greater honor and greater power: to forgive sins or to divide estates? (DC 1.7)

Anyone who is familiar with church history knows that the church's leadership has often gotten caught up in secular affairs to the neglect of spiritual matters. Indeed, worldliness and corruption in the hierarchy were no small factor in the emergence of the Protestant Reformation in the sixteenth century. It is no accident that Martin Luther later quoted this treatise of Bernard in an effort to call the pope of his day to reform.

But this is not just a problem for formal church leaders. All Christians face the dilemma of not letting worldly concerns so consume us that we do not pay sufficient attention to the things that really matter: the love of God and neighbor. Bernard's antidote to this problem is "consideration." He quotes Psalm 45:11, "Be still and know that I am God," and comments: "This certainly is the essence of consideration." At this point, Bernard defines consideration as taking time out to pray and to think things through before acting upon them. He goes on to speak of consideration as taking part in an action "by anticipating and planning what must be done" (DC 1.8). Thus, he treats it here as a kind of discernment, which he connects with the virtues of prudence, justice, fortitude, and temperance.

Turning back to the practical, Bernard advises Eugene to devote his personal attention to cases that will benefit the downtrodden:

Everywhere the powerful oppress the poor. We cannot abandon the downtrodden; we cannot refuse judgment to those who suffer injustice. . . . The case of a widow requires your attention, likewise the case of a poor man and of one who has no means to pay. (DC 1.13)

Other cases should be delegated. Bernard speaks with special disdain of arrogant and ambitious people who demand a hearing. He advises Eugene to refuse to give in to their demands.

This was certainly a tall order for Eugene, just as it is for anyone in a decision-making capacity today. It is much easier to pay attention to those who make the most noise, insist on their rights, and demand that they be heard. Very often, the people most worthy of our attention are the ones we ignore, because they do not have the resources to advocate on their own behalf. Bernard's advice here almost sounds like the "preferential option for the poor" proclaimed by today's liberation theologians.

Book Two: Consideration in Eugene's Own Life

Bernard begins book two with a reflection on the failure of the Second Crusade. If book one dealt with the consideration one must give to an action prior to its execution, book two begins by looking back at an action that has already been completed, and a disastrous one at that. We have already seen in chapter 1 what Bernard has to say about this. Suffice it to say that despite his defensiveness about preaching the crusade only because he was asked to, Bernard does seem to recognize that he needs to bear some of the responsibility for its failure.

Bernard now begins a more detailed examination of the term "consideration":

I do not want it to be understood as entirely synonymous with contemplation, because the latter concerns more what is known about something while consideration pertains more to the investigation of what is unknown. Consequently, contemplation can be defined as the true and sure intuition of the mind concerning something, or the apprehension of truth without doubt. Consideration, on the other hand, can be defined as thought searching for truth, or the searching of a mind to discover truth. (DC 2.5)

In other words, consideration has to do with discerning the truth in situations where it is difficult to grasp, by which he means the rough and tumble of everyday life. Bernard proposes to treat consideration under four headings: the pope himself, what is below him (the church that is subject to his rule), what is around him (his household, the curia, and his immediate surroundings), and what is above him (the angels and God). The rest of book two deals with the first heading, and the other three books deal respectively with the others.

Looking then at Eugene's own life, Bernard first reminds his brother that he must be concerned about his own salvation (DC 2.6) and must not forget his "first profession," which is to be a monk. Why was Eugene, who would have been content to remain in the monastery, elected to the papacy? Bernard's answer is direct:

Not, in my opinion, to rule. For the Prophet [Jeremiah], when he was raised to a similar position, heard, "So that you can root up and destroy, plunder and put to flight, build and plant." Which of these rings of arrogance? Spiritual labor is better expressed by the metaphor of a sweating peasant. And, therefore, we will understand ourselves better if we realize that a ministry has been imposed upon us rather than a dominion bestowed. (DC 2.9)

Bernard hammers away at this idea that the ministry bequeathed to Eugene is not one of dominion but of service:

This is the precedent established by the Apostles: dominion is forbidden, ministry is imposed. This is confirmed by the example of the Lawgiver himself who adds, "But I am among you as one who serves." Who would think himself without glory if he possessed that title which the Lord of glory first applied to himself? (DC 2.11).

Eugene should therefore glory in the apostles and above all in the cross of Christ. He should serve the church with responsibility and humility (DC 2.12), not with a desire to control. How often has this piece of advice gone unheeded in the history of the institutional church?

Bernard goes on to exhort Eugene to know himself, both his talents and his limitations:

Even though there are things which you can justly be pleased with, look at yourself closely and see if there is anything which ought to displease you. I want you to glory in the testimony of your conscience, but I also want you to be humbled by it. Rarely can a person say, "I hold nothing against myself." . . . They are totally deficient who think they are in no way deficient. (DC 2.14)

It should be clear by now that what Bernard is doing here is applying the teaching on humility that we have seen in his other works. Bernard also connects humility with his teaching on the Christian life as process, for he asks Eugene, "How will you continue to make progress if you are already satisfied with yourself?" (DC 2.14).

Bernard makes no bones about the papacy's exalted status. He thinks of it as having a greater dignity than all other ministries in the church. He says to Eugene, "You are the one shepherd not only of all the sheep, but of all the shepherds" (DC 2.15). He speaks of Eugene's call to the "fullness of power" and of being entrusted with the care of the universal church (DC 2.16).

However, lest this be seen as an occasion for pride, Bernard immediately returns to what kind of person Eugene is:

You were born a man; you were elected a pope, you were not transformed into a pope. Your humanity has not been cast aside; the papacy has been added. . . . There is a useful connection between thinking of yourself as Supreme Pontiff and paying equal attention to the vile dust which you not only were, but are. (DC 2.17–18)

Thus, Bernard calls for a balance in Eugene's assessment of himself. In a similar way, he advises him to act according to the principle of moderation:

Stand firm in yourself. Do not fall lower, do not rise higher. Do not proceed to greater length; do not stretch out to greater width. Hold to the middle if you do not want to lose the mean. The middle ground is safe. The middle is the seat of the mean, and the mean is virtue. (DC 2.19)

Bernard concludes by reminding Eugene that he should always look at himself from God's perspective. This means recognizing that all goodness within himself is a gift, while evil is his own doing. He needs to be vigilant about whether or not he is growing in the ways he should:

Distinguish carefully what kind of person you are by the gift of God, and let there be no deceit in your spirit. But there will be unless you faithfully discern and honestly assign what is yours to yourself and what is God's to God. I do not doubt that you are convinced that evil is your own doing, but good comes from the Lord. Now, clearly, when you consider what kind of person you are, you must also recall what kind of person you were. Later things must be compared with earlier: have you grown in virtue, in wisdom, in understanding, in agreeableness of character, or, God forbid, have you perhaps grown weaker in these? (DC 2.20)

Whether or not we are in a position of church leadership, are not these words of Bernard applicable to all of us? Don't we all need to recognize our fundamental call to humble service of one another? Don't we all need to take an honest look at ourselves and face both our talents and our limitations? Don't we all need to remember that our Christian life is a process or journey, and that we should never stop growing in our life of faith?

Book Three: Eugene's Subjects in the Church

Some of what Bernard says in book three has already been hinted at or stated earlier in the treatise. Indeed, what is most interesting in the next two books is to see what themes keep repeating themselves.

The first theme that reappears in book three is the call to stewardship and not domination. Bernard states,

It seems to me that you have been entrusted with stewardship over the world, not given possession of it. If you proceed to usurp possession of it, he contradicts you who says, "The world and its fullness are mine." . . . [T]here is no poison more dangerous for you, no sword more deadly, than the passion to rule. Certainly, you may attribute much to yourself, but unless you are greatly deceived you will not think that you have received anything more than stewardship from the great Apostles. (DC 3.1.2)

Bernard proceeds to reflect on the enormous task that lies before Eugene. He is called to convert unbelievers and to correct heretics. But Bernard sees an even bigger task for Eugene in rooting out the ambition that is running rampant in the church:

For even while we are in the Church we seek our own and envying one another and provoking one another we are stirred to hatred, aroused in injuries, excited to arguments; we mock deceitfully, we are quick to slander, we burst out in cursing, we are oppressed by the stronger and we in turn oppress those who are weaker. . . . Today, is it not rather ambition than devotion that wears down the doorsteps of the Apostles? . . . It is one thing for appeal to be made to you by the oppressed, but another for ambition to strive to rule the Church through you. You must not be inaccessible to the former, nor must you in any way give in to the latter. (DC 3.5)

In this connection, Bernard turns again to the issue of appeals. He pleads with Eugene to use his power of hearing appeals to liberate the oppressed and call oppressors to repentance:

What could be as fitting as this? that the invocation of your name liberates the oppressed and leaves the crafty with no refuge? On the other hand, what could be so perverse, so far from right as this? that he who has done evil rejoices, and he who bore it is needlessly harassed? . . . . Let the one man be consoled by the recovery of his losses, satisfaction for his injuries and an end of the false statements made against him. Let the other one be dealt with so that he repents of having done what he did not fear to do, and so that he cannot mock the punishment of the innocent. (DC 3.6)

Bernard's principle for a legitimate appeal is simple: "every appeal is iniquitous which is not the result of an injustice" (DC 3.7).

Bernard spends much of the rest of this book arguing that Eugene needs to make sure that proper jurisdiction is maintained in the church. He criticizes church officials for wanting to be independent and refusing to submit to the authority of their superiors (DC 3.14). Bernard reminds Eugene that his power is from God (DC 3.17) and that his task is to keep everything in proper order (DC 3.19). Bernard is convinced that the hierarchical order in the church is willed by God and parallels the heavenly hierarchy:

Just as in heaven the Seraphim and Cherubim, and each of the other ranks, down to the angels and archangels, are arranged under one hand, God; likewise, here on earth the primates or patriarchs, archbishops, bishops, priests or abbots, and all the rest are arranged under one supreme Pontiff. It must not be thought insignificant that this order has God as its author, and derives its origins from heaven. But if a bishop should say, "I do not want to be under the archbishop," or an abbot, "I do not want to obey the bishop," this is not from heaven. (DC 3.18)

Obviously, not all Christians would agree that a hierarchical structure for the church was willed by God. However, Bernard's remarks can still be seen as valuable. I am sure we have all experienced the problem of Christians who do not want to submit to any authority, who in effect make themselves the pope and will not listen to the wisdom of the community. In our freedom-obsessed culture today, no one wants to be controlled, no one wants to be under the authority of anyone. However, mature Christians do not see themselves as "lone rangers" but as members of the body of Christ. Therefore they see a value to authority as long as it is legitimately exercised, according to a model of humble service such as is promoted here by Bernard.

Book Four: Eugene's Household and Surroundings

Bernard begins book four on the same note that he ended book three, with a concern for proper church order. He starts with the clergy who are in Eugene's company:

These clergy should be very well ordered, for they especially set the example for clergy throughout the whole Church. . . . It is important for the glory of your holiness that those whom you have in your sight be ordered and organized in such a way that they be a model and mirror of all honor and order. They above all others should be prompt in fulfilling their duties, worthy to administer the sacraments, concerned for the peoples' instruction, careful to maintain themselves in all purity. (DC 4.2)

In other words, clergy who enjoy the prestige of being close to the pope should consider themselves to have a greater, not a lesser, responsibility for giving witness through service. This can serve as a reminder to all of us that "to whom more is given, more is expected." Instead of enjoying the privileges of rank, we should consider any special status that we have as an opportunity to be of greater service to others.

Bernard then turns to a consideration of the Roman people. What he says is not very flattering:

What has been so well known to the ages as the arrogance and the obstinacy of the Romans? They are a people unaccustomed to peace, given to tumult; people rough and intractable even today and unable to be subdued except when they no longer have the means to resist. (DC 4.2)

How should Eugene respond to this sad reality? Once again, Bernard sounds a note of moderation, advising Eugene to do the best he can, realizing that he alone cannot solve the problem:

Do not despair: care is required of you, not a cure. . . . [Y]ou do your part and God will take care of his satisfactorily without your worry and anxiety. Plant, water, be concerned, and you have done your part. (DC 4.2)

Bernard calls to mind Eugene's predecessors who can serve for him as an example:

They were not self-seeking but unsparing, unsparing of their care, their wealth, and themselves. . . . The only profit they sought from their subjects, their only glory, their only desire, was in some way to be able to prepare them as perfect people for the Lord. They devoted every effort to this, even in great suffering of heart and body, in labor and hardship, in hunger and thirst, in cold and nakedness. (DC 4.3)

Bernard laments that Eugene's contemporaries do not want to benefit from this kind of teaching and witness. He notes, "few look to the mouth of the lawgiver, all look to his hands" (DC 4.4). So many are only interested in taking and not in giving; they want to provide for their own insatiable desires while neglecting the poor. They even want the pope himself to pay more attention to honor than to holiness:

You see the entire zeal of the Church burn solely to protect its dignity. Everything is given to honor, little or nothing to sanctity. If, when circumstances require, you should try to act a little more humbly and so present yourself as more approachable, they say, "Heaven forbid! It is not fitting; it does not suit the times; it is unbecoming to your majesty; remember the position you hold." Pleasing God is their very last concern. (DC 4.5)

Bernard counsels Eugene to hold fast to his convictions. As his ultimate model, he urges the pontiff to follow the example of Peter, the poor shepherd, and not of Constantine, the powerful Roman emperor. Above all, he urges Eugene not to give up, for it is always possible that God will bring this hard-hearted people around (DC 4.8).

In our own day, all of us have to live and work in religious communities that are sometimes less than ideal and with people who can make our lives difficult. Bernard's recommendations in the face of these realities are as relevant today as they ever were. We should strive as best we can to call one another to conversion, but not despair when we can't do everything. Sometimes we imagine that we ourselves have to save the world; Bernard reminds us that it is God who will do the saving. Above all, we need to maintain our own integrity and always make our relationship with God our highest priority. Pleasing God should be our first, not our last, concern.

Bernard next offers some advice on the kind of people Eugene should choose as his assistants. The main qualification is wisdom:

It is your duty to follow Moses' example and to summon from everywhere, and to associate with yourself, not youths, but elders, men who are old not so much in age but in virtue, men whom you recognize as the elders of the people. (DC 4.9)

Thus, Eugene should screen people carefully before offering a position to anyone. Appointing someone to the curia is not the same as admitting someone into the monastery:

Therefore, if possible, proven men should be chosen and not those who have yet to be proven. We in the monasteries accept all men with the hope of improving them;

but the Curia usually accepts good men more easily than it makes men good. (DC 4.11)

Bernard notes that the best candidates for office are those who are not looking for the job:

Therefore, take in not those who wish office or who run after it, but those who hesitate and those who decline it; even force them and compel them to enter. . . . They are men of suitable character, proven sanctity, ready obedience, and quiet patience. They are subject to discipline, severe in censuring, catholic in faith, faithful in service, inclined toward peace, and desirous of unity. (DC 4.12)

How true this is even in the church today! People who want a leadership position so badly that they can taste it are often the worst leaders, insisting on their own prerogatives while attempting to control others. Bernard is a good judge of human behavior here.

Finally, Bernard speaks of how Eugene should preside over his household. He urges him to delegate as much as possible so that he can concentrate on the spiritual. Bernard criticizes church leaders who get too wrapped up in the minute details of administration:

Each day we carefully review the expenses of the day, but are unaware of the continual losses of the Lord's flock. There is a daily dispute with the servants concerning the price of food and the number of loaves of bread; rarely indeed is a meeting convened with the priests concerning the people's sins. An ass falls and there is someone to raise her up; a soul perishes and there is no one who gives it a thought. (DC 4.20)

Bernard recognizes that sometimes Eugene will have to get involved in the affairs of the papal household. As a rule of thumb, he again offers his advice that "in all things moderation is best. I would not want you to be too strict or too lax" (DC 4.22).

Bernard ends by reminding Eugene that his leadership must be rooted in solidarity with his people, clergy and laity alike:

Before everything else, you should consider that the Holy Roman Church, over which God has established you as head, is the mother of churches, not the mistress; furthermore, that you are not the lord of bishops, but one of them, and the brother of those who love God and the companion of those who fear him. (DC 4.23)

Thus, Bernard returns to his original answer to the question of why Eugene was chosen to be pope: not to rule, but to be of service to the church. Although he enjoys a unique position of authority as the Roman pontiff, he does so as a brother among brothers and sisters. All who have positions of leadership in the church would do well to remind themselves of this daily.

Book Five: Eugene's Relationship to the Things Above

In his first four books, Bernard speaks mostly of the consideration of things that need to be acted upon by Eugene. In this final book, he tells Eugene he will deal with "consideration alone, for those things which are above you, our present topic, require not action, but examination" (DC 5.1). That this book is the longest of the five is no accident. Remember, what is most important for Bernard is our becoming one spirit with God (1 Corinthians 6:17). Thus, in this book Bernard reflects on the heavenly realm.

We already saw in book three that Bernard sees the hierarchical structure of the church as willed by God and as parallel to the structure of the heavenly realm. Here he launches into a description of the various levels of the celestial hierarchy: angels, archangels, virtues, powers, principalities, dominions, thrones, cherubim, and seraphim. Bernard sees each of these beings as successively higher in the divine order. Thus, angels are closest to human beings, and the seraphim are closest in order to God (DC 5.8).

What is significant is that all of these heavenly beings reveal aspects of the wonderful qualities of God. To give just a few examples:

In these who are called Seraphim we can perceive how he loves who has nothing to elicit his love but who does not hate anything which he has made; we can perceive how he supports those whom he has made to be saved, how he carries them forward, how he embraces them, how that fire [with which the Seraphim burn] consumes the youthful sins of the elect and the chaff of their ignorance, purging it and rendering it worthy of his love. . . . Finally we can see and admire in the Angels and Archangels the truth and the proof of that saying, "For he cares about us" [1 Peter 5:7]. He does not cease to delight us with visits from such great beings, to instruct us by their revelations, to admonish us by their suggestions and to comfort us by their zeal. (DC 5.10)

Thus, all of the heavenly beings reveal aspects of God's goodness and love. Bernard makes it clear, however, that they are not substitutes for God's own presence and power in our lives. Thus, in comparing an angel's role to God's, he says:

The Angel is within a man suggesting the good, not effecting it; he is in us urging us toward the good, not creating it. God is present in a man in such a way that he causes an effect, so that he infuses or rather is infused and partaken of; this occurs in such a way that someone need not fear to say that God is one spirit with our spirit, even if he is not one person or one substance with us. Indeed, you have the statement, "Who adheres to God is one spirit with him." Therefore, the Angel is with the soul; God is in the soul. The Angel is in the soul as its companion, God as its life. (DC 5.12)

Bernard now turns to the contemplation of God. He speaks of God as the absolute beginning and author of all things, who created the world out of nothing and is incomprehensible (DC 5.13–14). Bernard focuses particularly on God's oneness:

Many things are said to be in God, and surely this is a true and Catholic statement, but the many are one. Otherwise, if we were to think of them as separate, we have not a four-fold divinity, but a hundred-fold. For example, we say God is great, good, just, and innumerable other such things, but unless you consider all as one in God and with God, you will have a multiple God. (DC 5.15)

This oneness signifies the purity and eternal sameness of God.

At the same time, Bernard declares that God is Trinity. He insists that this does not contradict what he has just said about unity, but rather it establishes "what the unity is" (DC 5.17). Bernard marvels over the mystery of there being three persons in one God. He finally exclaims that this can only be grasped in faith:

Does anyone ask how this is possible? Let it suffice for him to believe this, not as something evident from reason, nor wavering with opinion, but as something certified by faith. This is a great mystery, to be worshipped, not investigated. How can plurality exist in unity and in such a unity, and this unity in plurality? To scrutinize this is temerity; to believe it is piety; to know it is life, even eternal life. (DC 5.18)

Bernard compares this unity to other kinds of unity that are more familiar, such as "the unity of desire when the soul, clinging to God with all its desires, is one spirit with him" (DC 5.18). He goes on to defend the doctrine of the unity of the soul and body in Christ (DC 5.20).

Bernard ends his treatise with a fourfold description of God that he bases on Ephesians 3:18: God is length, width, height, and depth. Again he insists that this does not nullify what he said earlier about the oneness of God, for this description has only been given for our understanding. "Divisions exist in our understanding, not in God" (DC 5.27).

Bernard connects the length of God with his eternity, the width of God with his charity, the height of God with his power and glory, and the depth of God with his wisdom (DC 5.28-29). It is only the person who attains sanctity who can comprehend these things, to the extent that they can be comprehended. Disputation alone will not suffice (DC 5.30). This relates to Bernard's belief that the only true knowledge of God is experiential knowledge; only one who loves God can truly know God.

Bernard speaks of four kinds of contemplation that correspond to these four attributes. Perseverance corresponds to length or eternity; fervor to width or charity; marvel to height or power; and fear to depth or wisdom. He concludes,

I think it is easy now to compare our four terms with those of the Apostle: for meditation on the promises encompasses length; remembrance of blessing encompasses width; contemplation of majesty, height; examination of judgments, depth. (DC 5.32)

For Bernard, there is nothing about God that does not intersect directly with the patterns of human knowing.

Bernard closes his remarks with a statement that summarizes much of his theology and spirituality:

He must still be sought who has not yet sufficiently been found and who cannot be sought too much; but he is perhaps more worthily sought and more easily found by prayer than by discussion. (DC 5.32)

More than anything else, what Eugene needs to "consider" is his relationship with the One Triune God. This relationship is more something to experience than to talk about, and there is no way to experience it too much.

Significance of the Treatise

In the *Five Books on Consideration*, Bernard shows us a way of integrating the highest spiritual concerns with some of the most mundane tasks and challenges of everyday life. I would suggest that it contains important insights for all Christians, as well as some that are particularly relevant to church leaders.

For all Christians, the following questions emerge from the treatise:

1. How often am I more interested in my own gain than in the common good? Am I more concerned about defending my own rights and privileges than in reaching out to those in need?

2. Am I willing to take a stand against oppression, to challenge the rich and powerful to conversion, and to focus my attention on service to and advocacy for the poor?

3. How well do I really know myself? Do I honestly face up to my strengths and my weaknesses? Do I accept my limitations and realize that it is not I, but God, who saves?

4. Do I recognize my need to continue to grow and not become spiritually stagnant?

5. Do I keep focused on my relationship with the One and Triune God, who created and sustains me?

For someone in a position of church leadership, the treatise raises additional questions:

1. Is my approach to ministry one of domination or service? Do I sometimes abuse my authority in order to control people? Do I see myself in solidarity with my brothers and sisters in faith, or do I think of myself as being "above" them? Do I recognize my position of leadership as calling me to special responsibility and not the enjoyment of privilege?

2. Are my concerns primarily political or pastoral? How much time do I devote to administration as opposed to serving and being present to my community?

3. Do I align myself with the rich and the powerful, or do I challenge the structures of injustice and commit myself to defending and advocating for the poor?

4. Do I choose wise people as my advisors and confidants, people who are not afraid to challenge me where I might need to be challenged, or do I seek to surround myself with associates who tell me what I want to hear?

5. Do I take the time I need to nurture my relationship with God? Is the search for God my utmost concern?

In the end, the desire for God should be the most important thing in any Christian's life. If we grow in that spiritual union, everything else will fall into place, no matter how mundane. To make this our highest "consideration" is the ultimate challenge for all Christians, and it is a lifelong task.

Conclusion

Bernard's Legacy

There is no question that during his lifetime Bernard developed a widespread reputation as a monk, theologian, mystic, and statesman. But what is perhaps even more impressive is how strong an influence he continued to have on Christian life and spirituality long after his death. Indeed, that influence persists to this day.

Bernard of Clairvaux was canonized a saint by Pope Alexander III in 1174. As early as the thirteenth century, he was recognized as one of the "fathers of the church," and he has been quoted extensively by later theological and mystical authors, both Catholic and Protestant. He was declared a Doctor of the Church by Pope Pius VIII in 1830, a recognition that he is counted among the church's premier teachers and expositors of the faith.

The twentieth century saw the completion of a critical edition of Bernard's works, edited by Jean Leclercq and Henri Rochais. This led to the publication of new translations of his major writings in most major languages; some of the fruits of this labor have been presented in the present volume. The year 1990, the nine-hundredth anniversary of Bernard's birth, saw the production of a plethora of new research about the ongoing significance of the life and writings of the abbot of Clairvaux. Interest in Bernard seems to be holding steady as we turn the corner into a new millennium.

The influence of Bernard down through the ages is so extensive that it would be impossible to present it in one volume, let alone one chapter of a book. Nevertheless, a brief survey of some highlights will give us a good idea of just how important a figure he has been in the history of Christian spirituality. We will end with a summary of Bernard's significance for today.

Bernard as a Theological Authority

The writers who cited Bernard and expressed appreciation for his ideas are many. They include such important thinkers as Meister Eckhart, John Tauler, and Henry Suso (the German Rhineland mystics), Martin Luther, John Calvin, and Blaise Pascal. We will focus here on Eckhart and Calvin.

Meister Eckhart was a fourteenth-century Dominican priest who is known for an approach to mysticism that was somewhat more daring than Bernard's. Specifically, Eckhart was willing to speak of both a relational and a kind of essential union of the believer with God. Eckhart often cites Bernard as an authority who confirmed his own theological positions on such subjects as the nature of God and the soul's relationship to God. What is interesting is that the majority of Eckhart's Bernardine citations are taken from the *Five Books on Consideration*, not from a more mystically oriented work like the *Sermons on the Song of Songs*. Eckhart quotes especially from book five, where Bernard stresses the oneness of God, one of Eckhart's favorite themes.

This tendency to refer to Bernard selectively is not unique to Eckhart. Other writers too appeal to Bernard as an authority to back up specific theological arguments. This is especially evident in the use of Bernard by the Protestant reformers. John Calvin, for example, makes several references to Bernard in support of his theological positions on issues like justification, grace, and the understanding of the human being in relation to God. In his earlier writings, Calvin expresses disagreement with Bernard on a few points, but the majority of his references to Bernard express agreement and appreciation.

What is particularly interesting about Calvin is the way he understands union with Christ for the Christian believer. He actually calls it "mystical union" (a term that Bernard does not use), and he conceives of it in a way very similar to Bernard: as a spiritual union, rooted in faith and expressed in active service of God and neighbor. Curiously, although he quotes Bernard's *Sermons on the Song of Songs* fairly often, he does not do so in recognition of the similarity of his conception of union with Bernard's. Thus, it would be problematic to state that Bernard's understanding of mystical union was an "influence" on Calvin. Perhaps there was some unconscious influence, but it was certainly not direct. It is better simply to say that their conceptions of mystical union show some significant parallels.

In addition to being quoted as a theological authority, Bernard was sometimes appealed to in his role as a church statesman. When Martin Luther wrote his famous 1520 treatise on *The Freedom of a Christian*, he prefaced it with an open letter to Pope Leo X, in which he defended his criticism of Rome by appealing to Bernard's example in giving advice to Pope Eugene.

Bernard as a Biblical Theologian

One of Bernard's most important contributions to the church has been as an interpreter of the Bible. While it would be incorrect to see him as an innovator of new interpretive methods, he certainly was creative in integrating the text of the scriptures with his own experience. In a unique way, Bernard saw the texts of scripture as supremely relevant to his own (and to everyone else's!) spiritual life.

We have seen how Bernard's writing is saturated with references to the scriptures. Indeed, there may be more references to biblical texts in Bernard's writings than can be definitively counted, for allusions to scripture seem to permeate almost every line of many of Bernard's works. Bernard does not ignore the literal sense of scripture, but he is most interested in its spiritual meaning, particularly how it relates to individual and communal religious experience. We saw this especially in his *Sermons on the Song of Songs*.

There are times when Bernard's scripture references are not exact or explicit. Sometimes it is unclear whether Bernard is even conscious of the connection he is making to a biblical text. Even when he claims to be quoting scripture exactly, he sometimes takes liberties with it, changing the order of words or combining different references in order to make a point. In all of this, he was careful not to impugn the traditional meaning of the text. But he saw himself, and indeed others in the church, as authorized to draw out the spiritual implications of the sacred writings. As he put it in one of his *Sermons on the Song of Songs*, his own purpose in expounding the scriptures was "not so much to explain words as to move hearts" (SC 16.1).

While scripture scholars today would not encourage us to interpret the Bible quite as Bernard did, there is no question that his love of scripture and his conviction that it is supremely relevant to our lives should be considered a cherished part of his legacy.

Bernard as a Spiritual Guide

As we move into a new millennium, I would suggest that Bernard's spirituality can continue to guide us in many ways. In the light of what has been presented in this volume, I would suggest the following as particularly important aspects of Bernard's spiritual legacy:

- his insistence that the only way truly to know God is to love God. As we have seen, Bernard thinks that purely intellectual knowledge of God is of little value. The knowledge that counts is the knowledge that flows from desire, and that leads us to gratitude and selfless love. This is an urgently needed insight in a society that is becoming increasingly cold, technological, and impersonal.
- his emphasis on the seriousness of sin and our radical need for God's mercy and forgiveness. This poses a direct challenge to a society that trivializes or denies the reality of sin. While Bernard prefers to focus more on the mercy of God than human sinfulness, he addresses head-on the damage that sin has done to human beings and insists that our first response to God's grace, and the prerequisite for moving forward spiritually, must be a recognition of our own sinfulness.
- his proclamation of true freedom as not simply the absence of external restraint, but as freedom *from* sin and *for* service to God and one another. In response to a society that does not want to deal with ethical boundaries, Bernard insists that only by being "bounded" by grace will we find the true freedom for which we so ardently long.
- his recognition that the Christian life is a pilgrimage and a process. In response to a society that is obsessed

with instant gratification and instant results, Bernard holds to the notion that there can be no such thing as instant holiness or instant conversion. It is impossible to love God enough or to reach spiritual perfection in this life. There is no "fast track" to spiritual growth.

- his conviction that we need to find a balance between action and contemplation. Most of us today lead very active lives, even in relation to our faith. We are constantly "doing" things, often important things that relate to serving one another. Bernard does not disparage the active life. At the same time, he gently calls us to make time for our relationship to God and to be open to the gift of a contemplative experience.

- his understanding of true love as a selfless love that flows from the love of God. To a society that often confuses lust with love or reduces love to sentimentality, Bernard offers an exalted vision of love that will lead us to a deep union with God and with one another.

In the end, what can we say about Bernard of Clairvaux? Although he is recognized as a saint, Bernard was not perfect. He did not always keep his spiritual priorities straight. He made some mistakes in dealing with people. He struggled to live a good Christian life, just as all of us do. Maybe that is finally what makes him attractive as a spiritual guide. His spiritual insights are not detached observations but are the fruit of a life of intense engagement with God and with other human beings. May his words and example continue to inspire us on our pilgrimage of faith.

Selected Bibliography

Primary Texts in Translation

Abelard, Peter. *The Story of Abelard's Adversities*. A translation with notes of the *Historia Calamitatum*, by M. J. T. Muckle. Toronto: Pontifical Institute of Medieval Studies, 1964.

Benedict, St. *The Rule of St. Benedict in English*. Edited by Timothy Fry, O.S.B. Collegeville, MN: Liturgical Press, 1982.

Bernard of Clairvaux. *Five Books on Consideration: Advice to a Pope*. Translated by John D. Anderson and Elizabeth T. Kennan. Cistercian Fathers Series 37. Kalamazoo, MI: Cistercian Publications, 1976.

_____. *Homilies in Praise of the Blessed Virgin Mary*. Translated by Marie-Bernard Saïd. Cistercian Fathers Series 18A. Kalamazoo, MI: Cistercian Publications, 1993.

_____. *The Letters of St. Bernard of Clairvaux*. Translated by Bruno Scott James. Kalamazoo, MI: Cistercian Publications, 1998.

_____. *On Loving God*. With an analytical commentary by Emero Stiegman. Cistercian Fathers Series 13B. Kalamazoo, MI: Cistercian Publications, 1995.

_____. *On the Song of Songs I*. Translated by Kilian Walsh, OSCO. Cistercian Fathers Series 4. Kalamazoo, MI: Cistercian Publications, 1981.

_____. *On the Song of Songs II*. Translated by Kilian Walsh, OSCO. Cistercian Fathers Series 7. Kalamazoo, MI: Cistercian Publications, 1983.

_____. *Treatises II: The Steps of Humility and Pride; On Loving God*. Translated by M. Basil Pennington, OSCO, and Robert Walton, OSB. Cistercian Fathers Series 13. Kalamazoo MI: Cistercian Publications, 1973.

_____. *Treatises III: On Grace and Free Choice; In Praise of the New Knighthood*. Translated by Daniel O'Donovan and Conrad Greenia. Cistercian Fathers Series 19. Kalamazoo, MI: Cistercian Publications, 1977.

William of St. Thierry et al. *St. Bernard of Clairvaux*. The story of his life as recorded in the *Vita prima Bernardi* by certain of his contemporaries, William of St. Thierry, Arnold of Bonnevaux, Geoffrey and Philip of Clairvaux, and Odo of Deuil. Translated by Geoffrey Webb and Adrian Walker. Westminster MD: Newman Press, 1960.

Secondary Sources

Bredero, Adriaan. *Bernard of Clairvaux: Between Cult and History*. Grand Rapids: Eerdmans, 1996.

Casey, Michael. *Athirst for God: Spiritual Desire in Bernard of Clairvaux's Sermons on the Song of Songs*. Cistercian Studies Series 77. Kalamazoo, MI: Cistercian Publications, 1988.

Dinzelbacher, Peter. *Bernhard von Clairvaux: Leben und Werk des berühmten Zisterzienzers*. Darmstadt: Wissenschaftliche Buchgesellschaft, 1998.

Elm, Kaspar, ed. *Bernhard von Clairvaux: Rezeption und Wirkung im Mittelalter und in der Neuzeit*. Wiesbaden: Harrassowitz, 1994.

Gilson, Etienne. *The Mystical Theology of St. Bernard*. Translated by A. H. C. Downes. (New York: Sheed and Ward, 1940.) Cistercian Studies Series 120. Kalamazoo, MI: Cistercian Publications, 1990.

Leclercq, Jean. *Bernard of Clairvaux and the Cistercian Spirit*. Translated by Claire Lavoie. Cistercian Studies Series 16. Kalamazoo, MI: Cistercian Publications, 1976.

_____. *The Love of Learning and the Desire for God: A Study of Monastic Culture*. 3rd ed. Translated by Catharine Misrahi. New York: Fordham University Press, 1982.

Lekai, Louis J. *The Cistercians: Ideals and Reality*. Kent, OH: Kent State University Press, 1977.

McGinn, Bernard. *The Growth of Mysticism: Gregory the Great through the 12th Century*, vol. 2 of *The Presence of God: A History of Western Christian Mysticism*. New York: Crossroad, 1994.

Sommerfeldt, John R. *The Spiritual Teachings of Bernard of Clairvaux*. Cistercian Fathers Series 125. Kalamazoo, MI: Cistercian Publications, 1991.